trotman

The Daily Telegraph

The Insider's Guide to Applying to University

This first edition published in 2008 by Trotman Publishing, a division of Crimson Publishing Ltd., Westminster House, Kew Road, Richmond, Surrey TW9 2ND

© Trotman Publishing 2008

Author: Karla Fitzhugh

Designed by Andy Prior

British Library Cataloguing in Publication Data
A catalogue record for this book is available from the British Library

ISBN 978-1-84455-181-1

Typeset by Newgen Imaging Systems Pvt Ltd
Printed and bound in Great Britain by MPG Books Ltd, Bodmin

INSIDER'S GUIDE TO APPLYING TO UNIVERSITY

Contents

INTRODUCTION

So, you're thinking about applying to university or college. Well take it from us, it's a blackboard jungle out there.

But don't worry, because this book has been designed to help you see the wood from the trees, so you can pick the right courses and institutions. Your guides along the path are real-life applicants who have been there already, plus personal advisers and higher education staff – who are all ready to point you in the right direction.

This guide will help you to: research and make sense of confusing university and course information; work out how to shortlist courses and universities that suit your interests, skills and personality; and plan ways to increase the chances of your applications being successful. It will also show you how to complete the trickiest bits of application forms, and create a personal statement to wow the admissions tutors. There's even a section to make sure you'll survive and thrive during selection interviews and tests.

With a bit of luck you'll soon be accepting offers, but even if it doesn't go according to plan straight away there's still a second chance to win with UCAS Extra and the Clearing process if you follow all our tricks and tips.

What are you waiting for? Step right this way.

CHAPTER ONE
CHOOSING YOUR COURSE

Most students who are thinking about applying to university choose their subject or their course before they decide which institution they would like to study the course at. While some have a very clear idea of the direction they want to take, others need more time to think things through before they make their decision, and either way everyone needs to allow time for some reflection and do plenty of research. It's not something to rush, and the investment of effort and careful consideration can help you not only to pick the right course, but also to increase your chances of making a successful application.

As the financial burden of gaining a higher education qualification has increased greatly in the past few years, the quality of the degree and the employment prospects for its graduates have gained greater importance on the list of prospective students' priorities. Although funding and debt are both undoubtedly part of the equation, they shouldn't be the only basis for decision making. After all, you have to enjoy what, and hopefully where, you're studying as well.

There are many lists and tables that claim to tell you what the 'best' courses and universities are. These may be useful as part of gaining a broader overview, but should be taken with a pinch of salt on their own as the figures can be out of date or weighted according to criteria that aren't important to everyone. The best course for you is the one that you're most interested in, for your own personal reasons, and the only person who can decide that is you.

‘ In a nutshell, successful undergraduates are committed and genuinely interested in their subject. Openness to new ideas, trying out new things and socialising are also good. This doesn't mean you should join every society going; knowing yourself is really important. Be prepared to manage your own time and undertake a large proportion of self-directed study. **'**

FRASER SHADWELL, CONNEXIONS PERSONAL ADVISER

WHY GO INTO HIGHER EDUCATION?

Studying for a degree or diploma is an opportunity to explore an interesting subject in depth, and to challenge yourself intellectually. It allows you to push yourself and develop new skills, expand your horizons, increase your self-confidence, meet diverse and interesting people and expand your social life.

Studying can be hard work at times, taking you out of your comfort zone, but this can be rewarding in a variety of ways. Prospects for graduates tend to be better than prospects for non-graduates: people with degrees tend to earn more over their working life and are significantly less likely to be unemployed for any length of time. Certain careers also demand specific degrees or postgraduate qualifications before you can work in them.

COURSE CHOICE OVERVIEW

If you're certain that you want to go into higher education, the biggest decisions will be what to study, where to study it and how to fund yourself. This process can be quite complicated and time consuming, and sometimes it's difficult to know where to begin. It's easiest to break it down into smaller parts (see list below), so that you don't feel overwhelmed. Start by making a rough timetable for tackling each task, and create a progress file so you know where you are. You'll also be able to refer back to the file for reminders and pointers if you have moments where you get a bit lost or stuck.

Try breaking up your tasks as follows:

1	Think hard about your interests, talents and values
2	Look at broad subject areas that might suit you
3	Consider future career options
4	Narrow subject choices down into courses
5	Research course requirements, content, format and prospects

6   Check course standards, quality and ratings

7   Undertake extra activities to support your application

8   Match suitable courses with suitable environments

9   Start to apply for your chosen courses

10   Make applications for funding.

A recent survey suggests that up to a third of degree students say they chose the wrong course, and that picking a course or institution you find you don't like increases your chances of dropping out. Putting in some time and research into choosing the right course will allow you to be more confident in your decisions, and enjoy your course and surroundings. The more interested and happy you are, the more motivated you will be in your studies, which can gain you a better class of degree. Careful preparation pays off in the long run.

SEB KEITO, AGE 18, IS APPLYING FOR FIRST-YEAR ENTRY TO LOUGHBOROUGH UNIVERSITY TO STUDY CHEMISTRY.

'I had the best Chemistry teacher at secondary school, and he really started me off in thinking about doing Chemistry at Degree level . . . My family isn't very science based - but my sister is a chemist, and I read one of her chemistry magazines, and instantly I knew I wanted to do Chem by just looking at a molecule for anti-cancer treatment! I'm aiming to go into the pharmaceutical industry and become a Synthetic Organic Chemist (i.e. making medicines from scratch).'

'I find that doing A level Science subjects (Physics, Biology and Chemistry) I am extremely critical in my thinking. Anything that is problem based, I now work through it methodically and logically step by step. If I don't get the right answer, I'll start all over again and see where my mistakes lie. Chemistry is the basis for all of life and everything that we do today. Without it, we would not have medicines, no man-made objects - nothing.'

'To narrow my search down I looked at the RAE [Research Assessment Exercise] ratings of all the Chemistry departments, and their entry requirements and went on from there. I also needed my AS level results to see if Chemistry was my strongest subject, which, thankfully it is!'

WHERE DO YOUR INTERESTS LIE?

At this early stage, there's no need to worry if you aren't sure about what you'd most like to study. Even if you do have quite a firm idea of subjects you're keen on, or have a specific career in mind, some of the following pointers can help you to double check that you're going in the right direction.

The right subject, and perhaps career, for you takes into account the following factors:

- Your personality
- Your preferences
- Your talents and skills
- Your values.

> If you have decided that you want to go to university, but have absolutely no idea what subject or course to study, generally the best place to start would be to book an appointment with your local Personal Adviser through Connexions. They will be able to talk through your options with you and show you key resources. However, to get going straight away try "idea generators" such as the Stamford test on the UCAS website or the Higher Ideas demo (www.careersoft.co.uk/higherideas). Both are free and fairly easy to use.
>
> **NIKKI BRUNNING, CONNEXIONS PERSONAL ADVISER**

It isn't always easy being self-reflective but there are some exercises you can try to make it easier. For example, you could list your strengths and your weaknesses. Another interesting list to make is one of your interests versus dislikes. Gain extra perspective by asking several people who know you well where they think your strengths, weaknesses and talents lie. Yes, it can be an uncomfortable experience, and you might not always agree with everything others have to say about you, but they might come up with some striking observations that you hadn't expected, or good points you'd forgotten or were too modest to mention.

Ask a range of people for their opinions:

- Employers
- Family
- Friends
- Teachers, tutors.

Higher education advisers and careers advisers can be very helpful for bouncing ideas off, and can put you on the right path to find out reliable information. If you don't have a clue what to study or where you might end up, you could try some questionnaires and quizzes to identify sectors to research in greater detail.

Directgov and UCAS both recommend taking the **Stamford Test** (www.ucas.com/students/beforeyouapply/whattostudy/stamfordtest). This is an online questionnaire that asks you about your interests, attitudes and values. Depending on your responses to the questions, the test results make broad course suggestions. The objective of the test is to 'present a variety of courses in alignment with your stronger interests.' From these suggestions, you may discover several areas for further in-depth investigation. The questionnaire is easy to understand, quick to fill in and free to use.

Centigrade (www.centigradeonline.co.uk) is another test produced by the same people who created the Stamford test, to help you find the courses that will be suit you best. It is administered for free by some schools, or can be taken online for a fee of £15. It contains 150 questions and the results go into far greater detail than the Stamford Test. Some students find it useful, but others find the process a little 'mechanical' and strange.

UCAS also recommends **i-portfolio** (www.i-portfolio.co.uk), a website where you can take a series of personality tests and enter other details. The site then targets careers for you and allows you to access information from organisations such as UCAS and City & Guilds. It can also help you apply directly to certain courses.

When you're filling in questionnaires, don't say what you *think* you should say, just answer honestly about how things really make you feel. It's better if there's nobody looking over your shoulder. The results of these tests are only a jumping-off point to get your imagination going, and you don't have to follow all the suggestions. After that, the hard work really starts!

WHICH LEVEL OF QUALIFICATION?

The main qualifications covered in this book are:

- Three-year undergraduate degree courses leading to Bachelor of Arts, Bachelor of Science or Bachelor of Engineering awards. Most of these are with 'honours' to show the amount of work involved and the high level of specialisation.
- Four-year undergraduate degree courses, such as degrees in Scotland or sandwich degrees (with a year working in industry), leading to awards such as Bachelor of Arts or Bachelor of Science. These are also usually with honours (some Scottish universities describe these degrees as Master of Arts with honours).
- Two-year foundation courses (starting at 'year zero'), which prepare you for a vocation, or, on successful completion, allow you to gain entry into a relevant undergraduate degree course.
- Two-year courses leading to Higher National Diploma awards. If you complete the course with high enough grades, you can gain entry into the third year of a degree course.

INTEREST VERSUS VOCATION

By now, you might have more of an idea about the subjects that you want to study in higher education, or preferences for certain types of employment. You can learn more about either, and begin to slowly narrow the choices down. But not everyone manages to decide on a potential career at this stage, and if that includes you don't worry too much. You could look for a course of study that inspires you academically, or you may do a degree or diploma that's relatively general and won't drastically narrow down your career opportunities after graduation. Many graduate jobs don't ask for a particular degree, and some careers, including teaching and journalism, can be entered via a postgraduate diploma, for example. Meanwhile, all potential applicants should consider both subject profiles and career profiles to discover whether either approach suggests any appealing courses.

Subject profiles

Subject profiles can be a straightforward starting point from which to begin some general reading. They provide an overall feel for each general area, and give an overview of the individual courses that are available within each subject. The *Guardian* has a useful guide on its website (http://education.guardian.co.uk/chooseadegree) listing relevant courses that can feed into different career areas.

You can also look at over 50 subject benchmark statements provided by the Quality Assurance Agency (QAA) for higher education (www.qaa.ac.uk/academicinfrastructure/benchmark). To quote the QAA, 'Subject benchmark statements set out expectations about standards of degrees in a range of subject areas. They describe what gives a discipline its coherence and identity, and define what can be expected of a graduate in terms of the abilities and skills needed to develop understanding or competence in the subject.' These benchmarks are fairly flexible, and universities and colleges are able to adapt and customise their content.

You might wish to continue to study a subject you're already familiar with from school, college or evening classes. This has the advantage of being something you already know that you like or are good at, and it's a familiar area that you'd like to pursue in more depth. Otherwise you can choose a subject that's new, or based on an outside interest – there are many courses at university level that you don't get the opportunity to cover at AS or A level.

LAURA MCMILLAN, AGE 18, CURRENTLY AT ST THOMAS MORE SIXTH FORM, NORTH SHIELDS, APPLYING TO STUDY MA (HONS) ENGLISH LITERATURE AT THE UNIVERSITY OF GLASGOW

'Reading prose, poetry and drama interests me, especially more recently. As a child, who doesn't love being read a bedtime story? That is probably where it began, and now I enjoy reading absolutely everything, to criticise and to interpret. The degree choice I am heading towards taking will suit my personality perfectly. As an argumentative and analytical, critical person, I find Literature suits my want for continued learning. Literature can change your beliefs and attitudes to life, and that is what I like about it.

'I actually found it extremely hard to choose, I had wanted to pursue a different degree, but what I considered most useful was talking to people who had done a degree in either of the areas; I asked teachers of specific subjects whether or not they thought I had it in me to succeed in either. Ultimately, I have ended up going for English Literature because it is like my second skin. I believe I can push myself to my full potential if I continue in this degree.

'Despite struggling to decide on a course, I have always known that I want to study in Scotland. From there I looked at universities, and to do any of the Arts related subjects I've been interested in, Glasgow and Edinburgh came back as being the best choices. Glasgow felt more like home than Newcastle, where I live nearest to, and that in itself was a sign for my dedication to get into the University and onto the course. Ultimately, I have no specific career area I want to go into. As long as I get to use my skills and knowledge I will be happy with any area. Perhaps I will go into teaching.'

SINGLE OR COMBINED SUBJECTS?

If you're finding it hard to narrow your preferences down to a single subject, you could consider a course that combines two different subjects. Dual honours degrees are evenly split between two subject areas, often similar subjects, but occasionally quite diverse. You may also find degrees that offer two subjects as major and minor subjects, where 75% of the time and marks come from the major, and 25% from the minor. If you want to specialise in a certain subject, particularly if you want to go into postgraduate research, you will tend to be better off sticking to a single subject so that you can study the whole thing more comprehensively.

EXPLORING COURSES

To see the full range of available course titles in the UK, try the following services:

- **UCAS** provides a list of all full-time courses at universities and colleges in the UK that use its admissions service. To find out more visit www. ucas.com and use the Course Search function. This database is searchable by subjects or course codes, with the option to narrow your search by region, institution and type of course. The same full range of course listings are also available in the UCAS *Big Guide*, which contains the complete entry requirements for each one. Other sources of similar information include *Degree Course Offers* and *Choosing*

Your Degree Course and University, both by Brian Heap (published by Trotman).

- **Foundation degrees** are listed at the following webpage: http://develop.ucas.com/FDCourseSearch/Gateway.html.
- **Course Discover** is a searchable database of UK higher education courses. It is a subscription service that may be available via careers advisers or local libraries.
- For part-time degrees and diplomas look on **www.direct.gov.uk** for a database service powered by Learndirect.
- Some extra music courses can be found via the **Conservatoires Admission Service UK** (CUKAS) website (www.cukas.ac.uk/search/index.html).
- The **Department for Innovation, Universities & Skills** (DIUS) has a website (www.dfes.gov.uk/recogniseddukdegrees) of recognised UK degrees that you may wish to check out.
- The **British Council** also provides a complete listing of all official courses at universities and colleges in the UK via its website (www.educationuk.org).

Once you have prepared a shortlist of potentially suitable courses, you need to look thoroughly at the content and format of each course, to see whether it will interest you and suit your learning preferences. You should also carefully study the entry requirements for the courses that appeal to you the most, to gauge the chances of your application being successful.

COURSE CONTENT AND FORMAT

The content of a course, and the way it's organised and taught can vary greatly. In fact, two courses with the same name may be completely different, according to the institutions where they're being taught. Differences in content and format can make you love or hate a course, so pick with care. Consider which topics are likely to catch your eye and which ones might send you to sleep, and which course format you'll respond to the best.

There's no national curriculum for undergraduate courses, so they differ according to the staff teaching the course and location. For this reason, it's vital to find out exactly what you could be getting yourself into with every course you're considering. University and college websites and prospectuses often contain comprehensive information, including course content, teaching format and assessment methods. You can also contact the institutions directly by phone or email to ask for more details. They may be able to supply you with course brochures as well.

Courses that use the UCAS service may have a wide range of data included in their entry profiles on the UCAS website. Entry profiles may contain a list of required qualifications and personal characteristics, and a description of the institution's entry criteria. Some entry profiles are more complete than others, and some courses have no entry profile at all, in which case you may decide to contact the institution directly.

During the application process you will need to demonstrate knowledge of what the course contains, and how it's likely to be taught – this shows admissions staff that you're interested and motivated, and that your expectations of the course are realistic.

What should you consider with course content?

- Areas where you may need extra support or study
- Areas you could excel in
- How course content might relate to future careers
- Opportunities to specialise or gain work experience
- Sub-topics on the syllabus you're especially interested in
- Sub-topics you really can't stand
- The way the format changes throughout the years of the degree.

What should you consider with course formats?

- Flexibility (whether some parts are optional or compulsory)
- Hours of lectures, seminars and practicals per week
- How much independent study is required
- How the course is assessed: essays, reviews, presentations, projects, exams, continuous assessment
- How the marking structure is weighted
- Level of support from teaching staff

- Methods of teaching and learning you respond to best
- Time spent on work placement
- What key transferable skills will you learn?
- Whether the course is modular or non-modular.

SANDWICH COURSES

Many degree and Higher National Diploma courses are now being offered in the 'sandwich' format, which includes years of study at college combined with a year or more in industry, commerce or the social sector. Students earn a wage while they're working on placement, and may also gain sponsorship and go on to a full-time job with their placement firms when they graduate. Common formats include:

- The 'thick sandwich' – two years at college, followed by a year in industry, followed by a final year in college.
- A 1:3:1 course – one year in industry, three (or even four) years of study and a final year at a work placement.
- A 'thin sandwich' – the arrangement varies, but involves two six-month work placements, interspersed with time at college.

If you think this format might be right for you, details on all sandwich courses can be gained from the UCAS *Big Guide* book or their website (www.ucas. com), and from university websites and prospectuses.

ENTRY REQUIREMENTS

When you compare entry requirements for courses with similar titles and content, there is much variation between institutions. This variation should mainly be considered as a mark of relative popularity – the higher education entry process essentially functions as a market and the grades represent supply and demand. By raising entry requirements an oversubscribed institution hopes to be less swamped with applications, and by lowering requirements an under-subscribed institution hopes to increase its annual influx of applications and fill its course.

Degree course offers can make or break your applications. For every course you're considering applying to, you must go through the entry requirements as thoroughly as possible to make sure that you meet them. In addition to being asked for certain grades or points at A and AS levels, you may also have to have achieved high grades at GCSE in subjects such as Maths or English, produce certificates to prove you have been vaccinated against certain infections or that you have no criminal convictions, etc. It's all about reading the small print – failing to meet any of the compulsory requirements, however minor it might seem at the time, will make you ineligible for consideration and your application will automatically be declined, wasting one or more of your possible chances to get onto a course.

Entry requirements may also include writing essays for admissions tutors to assess, submission of portfolio or recent coursework, and the results of admission tests and interviews (see Chapter 6 for more details).

How are the points worked out?

Again, this varies from place to place and course to course. You may be asked for an overall set of grades at A level (such as AAB or CCC), or you may be required to attain certain marks in specific exams.

UCAS also operates a tariff system which aims to allow the comparison of different types of qualification, and puts a numerical value to levels and 'volumes' (amounts) of achievement. According to UCAS, the tariff works in the following way:

- Points can be aggregated from the different qualifications included in the tariff.
- There is no ceiling to the number of points which can be accumulated.
- There is no double counting – applicants cannot count the same or similar qualifications twice.
- Achievement at a lower level will be subsumed into the higher level, i.e. AS points will be subsumed into the A level points for the same subject. The same principle applies to Scottish Highers and Advanced Highers, VCE A levels and Double Awards, Key Skills and Music awards at different levels or grades.
- All certificated Key Skills in Application of Number, Communication and IT will attract points, whether achieved through proxy or not.

To find out more about the tariff system and tariff tables, visit www.ucas.com/ students/ucas_tariff.

For entry into some higher education courses, you may be able to use accreditation of prior learning (APL). It is the recognition of, and award of, academic credit on the basis of demonstrated learning (not just experience) that has occurred at some time in the past. There are different ways of calculating APL, so you are advised to check with individual course tutors if you think you might qualify.

Finding out about entry requirements

Two reliable sources of information are:

- The UCAS *Big Guide* – this is a book plus CD-ROM that contains complete entry requirements for all UK higher education courses using the UCAS tariff. The website (www.ucas.com) also has expanded entry profiles that explain more about the university or college offering the course, what the course entails and so on.
- *Degree Course Offers* by Brian Heap (published by Trotman) – this is a comprehensive guide to entry requirements that uses official information. It lists target grades and tariff points needed to gain entry to all UK courses, and also mentions teaching quality, research ratings, number of applicants per place (see below), graduate prospects, plus subject-specific advice for personal statements and interviews.

Although both of these guides are well respected, comprehensive and regularly updated, remember that university and college departments can readjust their average offers at any time. So don't assume you'll be made exactly the same offers as shown in the books.

Applicants per place

In addition to high entry grades, the number of applicants for each place on a course will help you to gauge how competitive it might be. The number varies considerably from institution to institution, depending on how popular the course (or perhaps the overall university) is. Don't be too put off if your favourite course has many applicants per place – if you feel you can get the grades and you have the right personality then you should at least give it a try. Some applicants pick one or more courses from their five options that aren't quite so competitive, as an insurance. You can find out the number of applicants per place at specific universities, by checking out the in-depth university profiles www.aimhigher.ac.uk, or on specific courses, by using *Degree Course Offers* by Brian Heap (published by Trotman) or UCAS's *Progression to . . .* series of subject guides.

Being realistic

While it's good to be ambitious, it's important not to apply to too many colleges and universities where you're unlikely to meet their conditions at exam time, in case you don't get in at all. Most applicants include at least one institution on their entry form that asks for lower grades or points, just in case exams results don't go according to plan, and also often include a choice where they're a iming slightly higher.

If your predicted grades are not high enough to get onto the courses you most want to study, your main options are to:

A   Take a chance and apply to at least one anyway (bearing in mind that competitive courses might not consider you), pick an insurance choice with lower entry requirements, then work as hard as you can to get the grades.

B   Wait until you've sat your exams, then – if you get the grades – apply through Clearing or for the following academic year (possibly taking a gap year in between). This can be risky so think about how much risk you're prepared to take.

C   Reconsider your choices and perhaps apply to the same course at institutions with lower entry requirements, or apply to other courses that are related or different, to increase your chances of getting in.

For option C, be aware that if you accept a place on one of the courses with lower entry requirements via UCAS, and then get higher grades than expected, you are still bound by UCAS rules to attend the course that you originally accepted. If you then decide to go for a different course with higher entry requirements, for example via Clearing, you will have to request the original institution to release you from your obligation. This can take time, and during this period all suitable Clearing places may become filled.

Only you can decide what to do, but take plenty of advice before following any specific course of action.

**MAHAMED ABUKAR, AGE 18, HAS RECENTLY FIRMLY ACCEPTED A PLACE ON
THE PHARMACEUTICAL SCIENCE COURSE AT KINGSTON UNIVERSITY**

'I've always been interested in Science, particularly the medicinal field. My interest occurred at the start of my GCSE year (year 10) and I noticed I did well in Science compared to other areas and I definitely enjoyed the practical and theory of Science. I'm not very good at Maths but I'm good at communicating science and helping people understand science. Before I applied for university I did have a Medical or Pharmaceutical course in mind.

'I did thorough research myself and found information on different types of scientific paths that lead to various areas in the healthcare industry. The UCAS website is also useful as they provide a test named the "Stamford test", which gives you a series of questions and the outcome of the test is a list of university courses you may want to think about. Also, emailing universities is a good thing and don't be afraid to ask anything; but if you think your question sounds daft then use an anonymous email address. Might I just add it's always good to be realistic; originally my intention was to do Medicine but looking at the grades needed (which where high) I chose an alternative course.

'I . . . thought of doing Biomedical Sciences (after deciding Medicine was very far from me) as that involves healthcare and medicines, but this course focused heavily on other areas of healthcare which didn't involve pharmaceutical science. It was too general for me. There were also a lot of universities offering Pharmaceutical Science but they did not offer the options which Kingston did. This course also offers other career paths relating to science so you don't necessarily have to enter a medicinal field.'

IMPROVING YOUR CHANCES

Once you have seen courses that interest you, and looked at their entry profiles and requirements, turn your thoughts to how you can attract the attention of admissions tutors and give your application the edge over the competition. Here are a few suggestions:

- Are entry requirements high, but you think you have a chance of meeting them? Let this motivate you to give even more attention to getting your grades if you're taking A levels, AS levels or equivalents. If your predicted grades aren't great, and you think you can do better, try to prove them wrong – higher grades can get you onto a top-quality degree course during Clearing, for example.

- If you haven't done too well in mock exams so far, and you have extenuating circumstances such as a bereavement or long period of illness, make sure this is made clear when you send off your applications. A supporting letter from a tutor, or a sympathetic reference stating your real potential can be a great help.

- Use course profiles to find out favoured personal characteristics and so on. Work out how you can demonstrate these characteristics on an application form or personal statement. For example, if you need to appear numerate, you could perhaps mention working as a cashier during summer holidays. To appear compassionate, you could arrange to do some volunteering or fundraising, and so on.

- If you haven't done so already, arrange relevant work experience, work shadowing, or even short visits to places of employment, especially if you're hoping to do a vocational degree. Make notes on what makes up an average working day, what might be challenging, and so on. Use it as a chance to ask lots of questions, and to make sure it isn't a profession you'd find dull or unpleasant.

ZOE ANDERSON, AGE 22, IS STUDYING FDSC FIELD ARCHAEOLOGY AT BOURNEMOUTH UNIVERSITY

'I've been interested in Archaeology since I was a little girl. I remember wanting to find everything out about the Vikings and Egyptians when we did school projects. I remember hiding my dad's tools in the garden and after a few weeks trying to find them again when I was eight years old. I'm a naturally curious person and I don't mind getting my hands dirty. I've always gotten excited when visiting historic sites, it seems like the right course to go for. I'd be happy in any archaeological career.

'Once I decided that I wanted to consider being an archaeologist I got in contact with universities and asked to volunteer at their excavations. I thoroughly enjoyed my experiences, and became determined to get into the field. I now have my own mini excavation and I teach the local school children the techniques of excavating and I have a secure place at University.

'I applied to Bradford and Glasgow as I had volunteered with their archaeology teams, Aberdeen because it was close to home, Leicester because of the research facilities for Archaeology, and Bournemouth because I was uncertain if my qualifications would allow be to enter at BSc level. If I apply myself I can get the chance to get placed on the BSc level of Field Archaeology and Bournemouth.'

NEWER SUBJECTS AND COURSES

In the past few years a diverse range of new subjects has appeared at degree and diploma level. They may be specific to emerging career paths, such as the renewable energy industry, or catering to specialist educational interests, such as rare languages. It could leave you at great advantage in a certain employment sector when you graduate, but beware of the 'teething troubles' with teaching methods, assessment and new curricula that can also plague new courses. These newer options might not be on the radar of some careers officers, so you must be prepared to do a lot of independent research if you're considering applying.

ACADEMIC STANDARDS AND QUALITY

'Academic standards' refers to how hard it is to gain a particular standard of degree (e.g. a first, a 2:2) at a college or university. Ideally, these standards should be similar across all institutions in the UK, even though their course content may vary. 'Academic quality' refers to how well courses are taught and assessed, and how well the students are supported.

The QAA advises UK higher education providers on both academic standards and academic quality. It provides external quality assurance in addition to the universities' own internal review mechanisms. Potential students will be most interested in the QAA's institutional review reports. These reports contain summaries of institutional and subject-level management, looking at areas of strengths and weaknesses. Further details can be found on the QAA website (www.qaa.ac.uk).

The Teaching Quality Information website was replaced by the **Unistats** website (www.unistats.com) in November 2007. This new website is run by UCAS and Hotcourses to help potential students and their advisers compare subjects (but not individual courses) at universities and colleges in the UK. The information is provided by the Higher Education Statistics Agency

(HESA) and the National Student Survey (run by the Higher Education Funding Council for England or HEFCE). It includes information on the following, searchable by subject and university:

- Student data – entry qualifications and UCAS points, continuation and achievement
- Destinations of Leavers from Higher Education (DLHE) data – destinations of leavers, job categories and job types
- Context statistics – student domicile, age, level of study, gender, study mode
- National Student Survey and student satisfaction.

☑ **TIP**

Reading up on a college or university's academic quality and academic standards can help you put together some intelligent questions to ask during open days or admissions interviews.

While there are government league tables for English primary and secondary schools, there are no such official classifications for higher education institutions. Some newspapers and other organisations produce their own league tables, but each one is based on different criteria and they rarely agree with one another. They can be useful to gain a wider picture, particularly when choosing which institution to study at, but shouldn't be used as the sole basis for decision making. League tables are covered in greater detail in Chapter 3.

RESEARCH RATINGS

Some people think that if a college or university produces excellent research, this attracts top-quality staff and provides a cutting edge learning environment for undergraduates. Others take the view that research staff may not necessarily be gifted teachers, or may not be able to devote much time to helping undergraduates. Research ratings do matter if you're thinking about going into research after completing an undergraduate degree, but otherwise they may not be the ideal deciding factor in picking the right course for you.

Every few years the HEFCE – in association with the Scottish Funding Council (SFC), the Higher Education Funding Council for Wales (HEFCW) and the Department for Employment and Learning, Northern Ireland (DEL) – conducts a Research Assessment Exercise (RAE) to judge the quality of research being carried out in UK colleges and universities. The current assessment is the 2008 edition, and the last complete set of statistics is from 2001. The results can be obtained from www.rae.ac.uk.

DROP-OUTS, SUCCESS AND SATISFACTION
Everyone wants to be on a course where they are likely to be motivated, happy and successful. Is it possible to gauge these variables?

Drop-out rates
Financial problems are given as the main reason for students dropping out of university in recent years. However, students sometimes leave their course because they're unhappy with the course content or the way it's organised and taught. Therefore these figures should be read with caution, preferably combined with levels of student satisfaction, as they don't tell the whole story. To look up drop-out rates, search for 'continuation rates' data on www.unistats.com. This will tell you how many students completed their course, how many left with no award, and how many are 'dormant'.

Success
In this instance 'success' means the number of students who passed their degree, and how many of them gained top classes of degree (i.e. firsts and upper second). This can be a measure of the calibre of the student intake, a measure of good teaching and student support, or occasionally it's a sign that the course is too easy. These figures should probably be viewed in combination with the entry grades a course requires, QAA ratings and student satisfaction.

Satisfaction
The National Student Survey results are also available on www.unistats.com, and they make for interesting reading. The main figure they provide is the percentage of students who say that they are satisfied with the quality of their course. The survey also covers areas of finer detail, such as teaching standards,

assessment and feedback, academic support, course organisation, learning resources and personal development.

CAREER PROSPECTS

It's relatively easy to find reliable statistics for university departments on how many of their students get graduate jobs within six months of completing their course, and the top 10 types of employment for graduates of a particular subject. You can also find out how many of the students are in further education, combining work with further study, or who are coyly described as 'presumed unemployed'. These DLHE data can be found arranged by institution and subject at the Unistats website (www.unistats.com). Be advised that this does not give statistics for individual courses.

If you want a greater level of detail, ask university department staff about which fields their graduates end up working in, and how many of them are in employment that directly relates to the course they have studied. These type of data do bear some relation to how vocational the degree was in the first place, so keep that in mind when making comparisons. You might also want to ask department staff about the transferable skills students can be expected to gain while they're studying, as this can ease the transition into many types of career.

Career profiles

The world of careers can be split into general 'families' or sub-groups, each with its own features and characteristics. Careers advisers will be able to suggest a range of books and leaflets if you decide that you'd like to browse through any of these categories. This is particularly recommended if you're thinking about doing a vocational degree, and it can sometimes be inspiring or serve as a reality check. The more you know about potential careers, the better are your chances of creating a successful application or doing well in an interview. Some fields of employment are also overseen by specific professional and regulatory bodies, and you may wish to contact them for extra advice.

Connexions Direct run **Jobs4U** (www.connexions-direct.com/jobs4u), a helpful website that allows you to research the full range of job families. Within these families it also lists many specific jobs and careers. There are hundreds of different job profiles (also accessible in a searchable A–Z format), detailing the required skills and qualifications, everyday life within that profession and salary expectations. There are suggestions for further reading and research, and you can also speak to a Connexions adviser.

You might also be interested in the career profiles on Learndirect (www. learndirect-advice.co.uk/helpwithyourcareer/jobprofiles/) and AimHigher (www.direct.gov.uk/en/Employment/Jobseekers/JobsAndCareers/DG_073361). www.aimhigher.ac.uk

The Graduate Prospects website (www.prospects.ac.uk) has a tool called **Prospects Planner** that allows you to look at what would motivate you in a job, identify your skills, generate job ideas and explore jobs in greater detail. It's mainly aimed at students in higher education and at recent graduates, but it can still help you explore a few ideas, especially if you have a fairly firm idea already of careers that you might want to pursue.

' If you have chosen a subject or course to study but have not chosen a career path remember that a lot of graduate level jobs are open to graduates of any discipline. It is important to separate out vocational and non-vocational degrees. For example, taking a degree in Music won't necessarily lead to work in this area, however it will give you many transferable skills. Another way is to research the employment destinations of graduates from subjects you are interested in. Take a look at the data on www.prospects. ac.uk and www.unistats.com. This is a complex decision and is also related to knowledge of the labour market and employment pattern; it would be prudent to ask for a guidance interview in addition to personal research. **'**
NAOMI ELFRED, CONNEXIONS PERSONAL ADVISER

DEFERMENT/GAP YEAR

Taking a gap year (deferring entry to university for a year) is becoming increasingly popular for a variety of reasons. Some people want a break from the pressures of studying, and others want the opportunity to explore the world around them while they're not tied down with jobs and mortgages. Other students use it to gain vital work experience that could give them the edge when they're applying for courses or future employment, and others are simply working to save up money so that they can fund their higher education.

A gap year can have a positive or negative effect depending on where you are planning to study afterwards. Tutors on longer courses, such as architecture, sometimes think that it causes too much delay, whereas others think it allows students to develop more maturity, skills and confidence. Views varies widely from department to department and even among tutors, so if you're considering a gap year you should discuss it with staff at the universities you're applying to, preferably well in advance. Ask whether there are any activities they especially value, such as extra learning, volunteering or specific types of work experience.

If you're considering having a gap year, think about how you're going to apply for a place at university or college. You can apply for deferred entry so that you already know you're coming back to start a degree at the end of the gap year – this has the advantage of being able to work closely with your school during the application period. Or you can apply to university during your gap year for entry that academic year – this has the advantage of you knowing your grades already so you don't have the uncertainty of waiting for conditional offers. University departments have their own preferences on this too, so check with them first.

A fruitful gap year takes some planning, especially if you're hoping to travel. You can make your own arrangements or join schemes where much of the organisation is done for you. Students often combine activities during the year rather than sticking to one thing, so they may spend some of the time being 'productive' (working, volunteering, learning) and some of the time being more leisurely (travelling, socialising, etc.).

You can start your research by:

- Chatting to other gap year students or arranging a trip on www. gapyear.com

- Learning about gap year perks and pitfalls on www.gapadvice.org
- Reading the Lonely Planet *Gap Year Book* by Charlotte Hindle and Joe Bindloss, or *Before You Go* by Tom Griffiths (published by Bloomsbury)
- Visiting a gap year fair, organised by Futurewise (www.myfuturewise. org.uk).

FUNDING YOUR STUDIES

Higher education can be expensive, but most students see it as an investment that allows them to pursue their studies, and hopefully to get a better job at the end of it. The funding and tuition fees landscape changes regularly, but you can keep abreast of it at Hotcourses Student Money (www.scholarship-search.org. uk), Directgov (www.direct.gov.uk; click on 'Education and Learning'/'University and Higher Education'/Student Finance) and HERO (www.hero.ac.uk/uk/ studying/funding_your_study263.cfm).

If you're lucky you may also be able to apply for scholarships or bursaries, and other funding you won't have to pay back. *University Scholarships, Awards and Bursaries* by Brian Heap (published by Trotman) is a comprehensive guide to universities and colleges offering extra financial support and sponsorships, and awards offered by professional, commercial and other organisations.

SUMMARY: COURSE CHOICE TIPS

1. **It takes time**. Be prepared to do a lot of research if you're looking for the right course, as there are so many variables, and lots of different resources you need to use to look up all the information. There are plenty of data available, but they aren't all found in the same place.

2. **Not everyone has a career in mind**. You may end up picking a subject that interests you, and taking it from there. You can collect subject- and course-related data to see what careers a course could lead you into, so don't worry too much at this stage.

3. **It's all about you**. Make sure that your course will fire your imagination and hold your interest, and make the best of your skills, talents and personality. Bounce your ideas off a wide range of people, and make lists and take personality quizzes.

4. **Content is key**. Two courses with the same name can contain very different topics and sub-topics. Be prepared to go into the finer detail when you're looking at what you might be learning about.

5. **Pick the right mode of study**. Only you can decide what course structure, teaching style, and amount of student-directed learning will suit you best. Again, it comes down to thoroughly researching your options and reading the course information's small print.

6. **Use official data**. Make sure you're doing a recognised course leading to an official qualification, and check out ratings for academic standards and quality. You may also wish to see research ratings, and read the results of the National Student Survey (see p. 20).

7. **What grades are needed?** You must balance optimism with realism when looking at course entry requirements – don't set your expectations too low, but at the same time consider what other options you might have if you don't get the grades you were hoping for.

8. **What does 'success' mean to you?** Whether it's completing your studies without dropping out, getting a first, or simply being happy with the teaching and organisation of your course and what you're learned from it, there are different ways to gauge how successful you might be.

9. **Start looking ahead**. You can also find out what your career prospects might be if you study a particular subject at a particular university. You can look at employment levels, and what types of jobs previous students have gone on to.

10. **Explore funding opportunities**. As higher education becomes ever more expensive, students need to consider additional sources of funding from loans, grants, bursaries, paid work experience and more.

CHAPTER TWO
COMMON MISCONCEPTIONS ABOUT COURSES

Once you get to the stage where you're looking at individual courses, you have to 'assume nothing and research everything' if you want to be successful. Too many people rush in without checking the small print, and the trained eye of an admissions tutor can spot this on an application form, in the wording of a personal statement or during an admissions interview. Fortunately, the right amount of preparation and focus can show them that you're genuinely interested and that you know what you're letting yourself in for.

' The content and structure of degrees vary so much between unis. English is a prime example. If the head of department has a specialist interest you need to check that the programme of study is not overly biased to this. If they offer a sandwich degree, are you responsible for work placements? Also remember that we all have our individual learning style preferences so it's important that students understand how they will be taught. In Medicine, for example, teaching methods and clinical contact can vary enormously between unis. '

FRASER SHADWELL, CONNEXIONS PERSONAL ADVISER

GENERAL MISCONCEPTIONS

Attention to detail is key when you are choosing between courses and selecting your favourite ones. Names and entry requirements can be confusing, and courses that superficially appear to be identical may well turn out to have little in common. Your personal preferences for course content and format, teaching style and modes of assessment make a big difference too, and can strongly affect your enjoyment of your studies. Make sure there are no nasty hidden surprises.

Entry requirements

Many applicants assume that you can tell the quality of a course simply by looking at the target offers that are made to applicants. However, this is a mistake. On their own, entry requirements say nothing specific about the course content or the teaching quality. The average target offer represents the popularity of a course more than anything else – higher education is a market, and the more popular courses raise their entry requirements so that they don't get swamped with too many applicants. The popularity of a course can come from the overall academic reputation of a university or college, or a department within it, rather than anything related to that particular course. People may also apply in huge numbers if they've heard that the university is in a party town or provides an amazing social life on campus.

The average conditional offers for courses are listed on various websites and in a variety of guidebooks (see Chapter 1). Remember that they are just guidelines, and are usually based on the previous year's figures. If a university or college really likes you, you may receive an unconditional offer anyway, or you may receive a conditional offer that asks you to obtain slightly lower grades. This could be as a result of performing very favourably at interview, for example.

Entry requirements may also be stated in points as part of a comparative overview, but in reality not all institutions use tariff points to gauge the potential of their applicants. Carefully research the entry criteria of any and all of the courses that you might apply to, as sometimes they are less straightforward than you might think. It's not always as simple as obtaining 'BBB' in your A levels, which is as it could appear in a table – you might need a minimum grade in a specific subject, or to have done very well in particular GCSEs first.

Confusion over course names

Course names can trip up plenty of applicants. Many have similar spellings in their titles but can land you in entirely different careers, for example, Pharmacology is not the same as Pharmacy, and will not help you to train as a pharmacist. Be extra-careful not to mix up courses with similar-sounding names, or to confuse course variations. There may also be specific words in a course title that give students the incorrect impression, so it's quite common for people to confuse a course such as theatre studies with gaining a performing arts place at drama school, and so on.

As always, reading through all the provided course information is necessary to dispel any myths or misleading ideas. Extra research also helps to create a more realistic picture, and asking the university questions when you get stuck is a good way to deal with confusion that might arise while you're reading their literature.

General course details

Some people tend to assume that courses with the same name will have the same content everywhere they are taught – but they are wrong. General course details are highly variable, and not finding out enough beforehand can lead to students hating their course and even dropping out. It's simply not something you can hope to second guess, so you must research the course content thoroughly and be clear about what you're applying for.

Your personal preferences are vital to consider when you're looking at degrees and other courses. What do you respond to best? Take careful note of the following variations:

- **Course structure**. Is this course split into discrete modules, or is it something more traditional and continuous? What do the major components consist of? Do you like the look of all of them? Which sub-topics are given the most weight on this course? How does the structure change over the years of study?
- **Course type**. Is the course being offered as single or dual honours? Are there major and minor subjects? Would you be expected to follow one subject closely, or study something broader and more multi-disciplinary?
- **Flexibility**. Can you take on extra subjects or drop some? What's compulsory? Do you actively dislike any compulsory subjects or modules that are listed? Is there room for specialisation later on during the course? Can you study additional topics that aren't related to your main subject?
- **Teaching style**. How many lectures are there per week, and how long is each one? Which staff do the lecturing? How much do they interact with the students? Are there seminars, tutorials, other presentations, guest speakers and so on? What other teaching methods are used?
- **Self-directed learning**. To what extent are students responsible for their own reading and research, and how many hours are allowed in the timetable for this? Do you like being left to take charge of your own

learning or do you prefer more guidance from staff? What support is provided to students to assist their self-directed learning?

- **Modes of assessment**. Is it continuous assessment or mainly exam-based? What format do exams take and when are they held? What proportion of marks are given for essays, practicals, reviews, presentations, work experience assessments, dissertations and so on? Do you do better in exams or would you do anything to avoid them?
- **Work experience opportunities or chance to travel abroad**. Is this optional or compulsory, and what do other students say about it? What's available to choose from? Where are you willing to go?
- **Career considerations**. Does the course comply with the regulations of the appropriate professional bodies? Are you certain that this is the qualification you must have to get into your chosen career? Is this qualification needed before you can pursue a particular postgraduate course or other qualification?

SUBJECT-SPECIFIC MISCONCEPTIONS

Many of the wrong ideas listed below come from people who haven't read prospectuses carefully enough. Occasionally, inaccurate beliefs are held by advisers too, which is a reminder of the importance of backing up your research and not taking everything you're told at face value.

Architecture

This course is more about design, rather than engineering.

Biomedical Sciences

This course does not qualify graduates to practise as medical doctors or nurses.

Building

Does not train students to become bricklayers or structural engineers.

Economics

This is not the same as taking a business studies course.

Education Studies

Graduates of this course are not qualified to work as teachers.

Film Studies

This is not a course that trains budding film-makers.

Food Science

This is not for someone who wants to train to become a chef.

Forestry

Does not train applicants to become lumberjacks.

History of Art

Students are not expected to produce their own artwork.

Languages

Applied language courses are not about the study of literature.

Media Studies

Will not train applicants for a specific job in the media, or to be journalists.

Music

This degree is not necessarily about being a performer.

Pharmacology and Pharmaceutical Science

This is not a pharmacy degree and will not qualify a graduate to work as a pharmacist.

Physiotherapy

This is not all about treating sports injuries.

Podiatry

An academic course that is more complicated than becoming a chiropodist or pedicurist.

Psychology

Does not train students to become psychotherapists or psychiatrists.

Radiography

Not to be confused with radiotherapy or radio production.

Religious studies

Not necessarily about Christianity, or any other specific religion.

Social and Public Policy and Administration

Doesn't provide students with a qualification in social work.

Sports Sciences

Not a course for training Olympic hopefuls or other athletes.

Theatre Studies

These courses should not be confused with stage school or performing arts courses.

Zoology

Not the same as Veterinary Medicine or Veterinary Science.

SUMMARY: SEVEN STEPS TO UNDERSTANDING COURSE INFORMATION

1. **Read the small print carefully**. Attention to detail makes all the difference when you're looking for the right course, and applying to one.

2. **Read *all* of the small print**. You don't just need some understanding, you need complete understanding of the important points. This helps at interview too.

3. **Don't jump to conclusions**. Not all courses are the same, even if they appear superficially similar, and you'll only find out by putting the groundwork in. Look before you leap.

4. **Take care with titles**. Similar titles can lead to entirely different degrees, qualifications and careers. Check spellings and key words.

5. **Respect entry requirements**. Make sure you meet all compulsory requirements for your application, or you'll run the risk of getting immediately rejected.

6. **Course details matter**. Content, format, teaching style and marking schemes vary widely between institutions. Your preferences are important, and can make the difference between thriving and being unhappy.

7. **Find out more**. If thorough research doesn't give you the answers you need, don't be scared to ask university staff any further questions you have. It also makes you look motivated.

CHAPTER THREE
CHOOSING YOUR INSTITUTION

If you've already found the right kind of course, now's the time to pick an institution that will allow you to pursue as many of your academic and other interests as possible, and that suits your personality.

' Your choice of higher education institution really is important. For most people university is also much more than just gaining a degree, and choices should be made on a wider basis. For example, what social activities are they offering? If you require learning support how is this delivered? Finally geography is a key consideration. How far do you want to be away from home, and is it campus based or urban? '
NIKKI BRUNNING, CONNEXIONS PERSONAL ADVISER

WHERE DO YOU START?

Researching universities and colleges is time well spent, so think of it as an investment. Your university environment has a huge effect on your quality of life, and if you're going to be there for a few years then it makes sense to look hard for the place where you'll be the happiest.

1   Think about the general environment you'd prefer

2   List your main requirements

3   Check university guidebooks and league tables

4   Go to higher education exhibitions and conventions

5   Look at official data

6   Read prospectuses and university websites

7 Quiz current and former students and staff

8 Make a shortlist of universities and colleges

9 Visit places on your shortlist on open days

10 Keep asking questions until you're certain.

THINGS YOU MIGHT WANT TO CONSIDER

There's much to take into account when you're deciding where to study. Try thinking about all of the following, and work out which points are likely to carry the most weight for you.

- Accommodation
- Age: traditional, 'red brick', newer college
- Amenities
- Atmosphere
- Campus or non-campus
- Chance to earn
- Cost of living
- Distance from home
- Extra requirements
- Graduate recruitment
- Green credentials
- Hobbies and interests
- Links to industry
- Mixture of students
- Reputation
- Setting
- Size, number of undergraduates
- Social life
- University opportunities outside your course
- What students say.

Accommodation

- Is university accommodation provided for the first year to all new students?
- Is it large traditional halls or smaller flats?

- How near is it to where you'll be studying?
- Do students have to share rooms, kitchens or bathrooms?
- Is it catered or self-catering?
- Are there common rooms, a bar, laundry facilities, cleaners, telephones?
- Is there internet access?
- What are the security arrangements?
- How safe it is walking around at night?
- Is there secure parking or bicycle storage?
- For students who do not stay in halls, what other accommodation is available?
- What condition is it in, how many share one dwelling on average, where are most of the properties, and how much do they cost?

Age: traditional, 'red brick', newer college

Would you like to go somewhere that's traditional and well established, and has a long history? Or would you be better off somewhere more modern, either in its buildings or its outlook or teaching methods? If a traditional university or college doesn't appeal to you, you might be happier at one of the further education colleges that have recently started to offer higher education courses.

Amenities

Academic resources to consider include the quality of the main and departmental libraries, lecture theatres and tutorial rooms, computer labs, science and other practical labs, copying and printing resources and so on. You might also want to look at sporting facilities, such as a running track, sports pitches, subsidised university gym or swimming pool. The institution may also have a busy students' union building, student health or counselling centre, a careers centre, an employment office, on-site cinema, places to eat, one or more bars, theatres, stages for bands to play, a nightclub, a bookshop, a stationery shop, etc.

Atmosphere

- Is the pace of life hectic, average or laid back?
- Is it noisy or quiet?
- Is there a 'buzz' about the whole place, or just the university, or certain departments? Is it formal or informal?

- Is the place in good condition or run down?
- Are people serious, fashionable, fun-loving, friendly, competitive?

Campus or non-campus

A campus university is one where the university teaching, accommodation and leisure facilities are usually grouped together in one place. They are often found in the outskirts of cities. Some of the more established campus universities have grown so large that they have one or more extra sites now. Non-campus (or collegiate) universities are often older and more traditional, tend to be based in a town or city, are much more spread out over different sites and may comprise different colleges. Occasionally, just to be confusing, the different sites of collegiate universities are sometimes referred to as campuses.

Chance to earn

Part-time work is a fact of life for many students. If you think you will need to work, check out the opportunities for paid work in the university and whether it has a job shop on campus. Try to find out how many students have part-time jobs and whether the work pays well or will you have to do loads of extra hours to make ends meet. What about nearby employers? It's also worth considering whether any of the jobs look good on your CV.

Cost of living

On top of your course costs, it's worth finding out about the general cost of living in the area. Ask around to see what rents and bills are like, and whether you can get cheap food, drink and entertainment. Transport costs are part of the equation too, from everyday getting around to trips back to see the family.

Distance from home

Sometimes it's good to strike out on your own, and explore a completely different environment for a few years. Or you may decide to stay closer to home to save on transport costs, be nearer to your existing social network, or keep an existing job and study a part-time degree.

Extra requirements

These can be anything from childcare facilities and financial support for students with children (start with www.direct.gov.uk and university websites), to accessibility and other issues for students with disabilities (try www.skill.org.uk or call their free helpline on 0800 328 5050).

Graduate recruitment

Although over a third of graduate recruiters say that they don't look for people who have studied at specific universities, some recruiters are influenced by the name (and hopefully also the recent performance) of the institution. Many recruiters from industry and commerce target some or all the following universities: Bath, Birmingham, Bristol, Brunel, Cambridge, Cardiff, Durham, Edinburgh, Exeter, Imperial College, Leeds, London School of Economics, Loughborough, Manchester, Nottingham, Oxford, Sheffield, Southampton, Warwick. This list varies from one employer to another, and if you have a specific career path in mind then you might want to research which universities are favoured by some of the big employers in that field.

Green credentials

If you're interested in places that are environmentally friendly or sustainable, you can have a look at the People & Planet's *Green League*. It's a controversial report that contains a league table of universities' environmental performances (http://peopleandplanet.org/gogreen).

You can also read the *Greening Spires* report produced by Universities UK (downloadable from: http://bookshop.universitiesuk.ac.uk/downloads/green_spires.pdf).

Hobbies and interests

You might be hoping to continue with some of your favourite hobbies, or you might like to take up some new ones. If you're the sporty type, do you want to get a bit of exercise and boost your social life, or could you cut it in an award-winning team or national event? Being a high achiever in a particular sport can give your application form the edge with some colleges and universities. You might need a certain environment too: rock climbers and hikers might like to be near the Peak District, for example, and surfers could be drawn to Cornwall. Or you may be more likely to be interested in somewhere that has a thriving arts, music or theatre scene, whether at the university or nearby.

Links to industry

Some universities and colleges have strong links to local businesses, while others are better connected with national and international employers. There may be opportunities to win sponsorships, to undertake work experience, and to gain paid part-time or holiday employment. There may also be graduate schemes and mentoring. These links are sometimes found through specific departments, and sometimes via the careers service.

Mixture of students

If you want to encounter a variety of other cultures and maybe improve your language skills, you can try a place with a high proportion of overseas students. Or you may be a mature student who wants to study somewhere that has a high intake of people your age. Or you might just be interested in the male–female ratio (I can't imagine why!). These types of statistics can be found on the UCAS website, which has information on most institutions.

Reputation

This can be quite tricky. While some universities are undoubtedly well known and hard to get into, such as Oxford, Cambridge, Edinburgh, Durham and so on, it doesn't mean that the course you want to do, the teaching style of that course or the department where the course is taught is particularly wonderful or will suit you. Also, a reputation, negative or positive, may linger for many years even if it is no longer accurate. Try to stick to recent data and experiences when making your mind up.

Setting

There really is something for everyone here. You can find yourself studying in a big metropolitan city, an industrial heartland, a large town, a picturesque small town, a campus in the middle of the countryside, or near to mountains, hiking country or the sea. Look areas up on maps to see how large they are, and what's nearby.

I picked my uni based on the location mostly. I did some research and found out most of the Biology courses with the grades I was predicted were pretty much the same, so I looked at the location and the campus. I realised I didn't want to live in a big city as I'm from the country so I'd feel a little lost, and York seemed like the perfect place, not too big yet not too small. I also liked the look of the flexibility of the course, giving me the chance to specialise in my interests, and the fact that York is one of the best in the country for Biology was just an added bonus really. **"**

**EMILY COOPER, AGE 18, ABOUT TO START HER FIRST YEAR
STUDYING BIOLOGY AT THE UNIVERSITY OF YORK**

Size, number of undergraduates

You may like to attend a smaller college or university, where you can get to know everyone. On the other hand it might make you feel like a big fish in a small pond. Or perhaps you'd prefer to go somewhere much larger where you can meet many more people, even though sometimes you might feel more anonymous or lost in the crowd. The number of people in your department and course year may be just as important as the overall size of the institution.

Social life

Depending on your preferences, you can pick somewhere relatively quiet, somewhere with a busy social scene based on campus, or a lively city or town with a busy nightlife. If you want to be extra sociable, look for a university or college that supports several clubs and societies.

University opportunities outside your course

Going to university is not only about getting good grades on your course. It's a chance to try new experiences and grow as a person, and potential employers are often just as interested in what you did at university that was non-course related. It's a chance to make new friends, push yourself, show commitment and responsibility, and learn many transferable skills. Your university may offer a variety of extra activities, including:

- Presentation skills training
- Research skills courses
- Learning new languages
- Information technology (IT) training

- Volunteering opportunities
- Conservation schemes
- Fundraising
- University paper, radio or television experience.

Some higher education institutions offer credits for some of these activities that can count towards the final level of your degree, so it's worth finding out whether your chosen college or university offers this credit accumulation and transfer (CAT). See www.nicats.ac.uk/about/cats_uk.htm to find out more.

What other students think

To gain the best idea of the whole student experience at a particular college or university, ask a cross-section of current students and recent graduates what the place is really like. These could be relatives, neighbours, student reviewers on www.whatuni.com, or students who use online message boards such as www.yougofurther.com, or www.thestudentroom.com. You can also view the results of student surveys, for example, the results of the annual National Student Survey (www.thestudentsurvey.com) can be found at Unistats (www.unistats.com).

RESEARCHING COLLEGES AND UNIVERSITIES

Once you've come up with a rough idea of the kind of place you would like to attend, make a shortlist of the things that are most important to you, as well as other features you'd quite like but which aren't essential. Next, use some of the many university guides, and perhaps league tables, to find several institutions that might fit your requirements. Remember at this early stage that nothing is set in stone; be prepared to be flexible and repeat steps if necessary.

University guides

There are many university guidebooks and websites. They are useful at this stage because they can give you quick access to summaries of lots of different institutions, so you can easily browse through to find several that interest you. Each guide has its own style and flavour, ranging from the deeply serious to the downright irreverent, and you may wish to refer to more than one to get a better combined overview.

- *Choosing Your Degree Course and University* by Brian Heap (published by Trotman) is a comprehensive guide for anyone who is unsure about what or where to study. It discusses types of degree, career aspirations, and teaching quality.
- *Student Book 2009* by Klaus Boehm and Jenny Lees-Spalding (published by Trotman) is a one-stop guide for applicants to UK universities and colleges. Contains over 250 university and college profiles and input from current students.
- *The Guardian University Guide*, edited by Donald Macleod, contains advice on what to study, where to go and how to get there. It includes student reports of what universities are like.
- *The PUSH Guide to Choosing a University* by Johnny Rich (published by Hodder Education) links in with an online system that allows students pick their top university by ranking their preferences.
- *The Times Good University Guide* by John O'Leary is quite technical and includes a lot of statistics. It evaluates the strengths and weaknesses of each university, and provides detailed information about getting into Oxford and Cambridge.
- *The Virgin Alternative Guide to British Universities* by Piers Dudgeon contains many contributions from students themselves, and gives a good sense of the true experience of studying at a particular institution.

League tables

Many newspapers publish league tables every year, each claiming to show you which institution is 'the best', or which course is 'the best'. The results often differ, as each league table is decided by weighting a range of different factors, not all of which will be a priority for you. Therefore, while they're useful for background research, you should not make any strong assumption after reading a single table. The data can be hard to interpret, but there's a UCAS publication, *How to Read League Tables*, that gives useful advice.

- The Good University Guide is only available online (www. thegooduniversityguide.org.uk). It allows you to customise your search by selecting your own criteria.
- The *Guardian* league tables are compiled by giving marks out of 10 for various factors, rather than presenting raw data. View the tables at http://education.guardian.co.uk/universityguide.

- *The Sunday Times* league tables are compiled in a different way, so you might like to view them too at www.timesonline.co.uk/tol/life_and_style/education/sunday_times_university_guide
- *The Times* league tables are found in *The Times Good University Guide*, and are also available online at www.timesonline.co.uk/tol/life_and_style/education/good_university_guide

Official statistics

So far, your search might probably have been quite general, and much of what you would have heard and read would have been fairly subjective since the writers and compilers of the information each have their own ideas about what's important and what's not. Treat them all with caution until you've double-checked a few of the important facts about the universities.

The UCAS Institution Guide (www.ucas.com/students/beforeyouapply/wheretostudy/instguide) covers the majority of courses and institutions in the UK. It provides reliable but basic information about student numbers, accommodation, location, campuses and so on. It also has contact details for all institutions and links to their websites so that you can continue your research.

The DIUS (www.dcsf.gov.uk/recognisedukdegrees/) lists all institutions in the UK that are recognised as degree-awarding universities and university colleges and provide courses that lead to recognised degrees. It also names listed institutions that offer courses leading to degrees that are awarded by recognised bodies. The information provided by the DIUS also feeds into the HERO/Aimhigher database, which is called 'Uni.finder'. This gives a brief profile of each institution, and its website and contact details.

If you want to read about institutions and the subjects they offer in greater depth you can try the British Council website (www.educationuk.org/pls/hot_bc/page_pls_all_homepage) for its Institution Search profiles. They have been written primarily for overseas students but are useful for all applicants.

University prospectuses, course-specific prospectuses and university websites usually contain most of the information you would be looking for, so collect as many as you want and read them thoroughly. Contact admissions staff for more information if needed. Remember that this is a marketing exercise for them to some extent, so while they are unlikely to give inaccurate information, they're only going to show themselves in the most positive light. Be prepared to do some more digging before you start to narrow down those options.

' Keele's prospectus was the first University prospectus I ever looked at to be honest, and though I still have a bag full of 15 others none of them really topped Keele. I like it because of the location, it's in the countryside so it won't be too much of a culture shock for me coming from a small town, but it's really easy to get into Newcastle-under-Lyme and Stoke if I'm looking for stuff to do, so it's the best of both worlds. The School of Politics, International Relations and Philosophy is also good and does a good Politics course which was an attraction for me. It also offers study abroad opportunities and because I've never been abroad I would love to do this. Not just for a holiday (honest!) but because it adds something extra to my degree and I would like to experience a different culture. '
SOPHIE W, AGE 18, DEBEN HIGH SCHOOL (SUFFOLK)

Talking to people

Take every chance you can to discuss possible colleges or universities with current and former students, or friends and relatives who have lived in those areas. Higher education advisers or careers counsellors may be able to give you ideas or recommend some reading. Bear in mind that some people might be a bit biased, or that their information may be out of date. Remember you can always email or phone the university if you want to double check information given to you by some else – don't be scared to ask questions, even if they seem a bit silly at the time.

Higher education conventions and fairs

UCAS runs over 50 conventions and fairs around the UK each year. Some are large central events for anyone who's interested in higher education, and others are more local. Most conventions are not subject-specific and attract exhibitors from all of the institutions that use UCAS to handle their applications.

Some have a narrower range of subjects, for example, they may be devoted to performing arts, design or the health professions. Conventions and fairs are an ideal opportunity to speak in depth with staff from a range of institutions all on the same day. They also attract other organisations such as student travel firms, professional bodies, student support services, Connexions staff and gap year organisations. Entry is free, and you can turn up without booking.

You will get the most out of a convention or fair if you have already done some preliminary research into what and where you would like to study. This should give you a 'hit list' of stands and staff to target, preferably with a pleasant smile and a few questions. Look at the programme before you arrive to see who is going to be there, and check for the timing of any interesting presentations or seminars. Pick up a floor plan of exhibitors at the front door as you arrive, which will allow you to decide on the quickest route to take to get around all the stands on your hit list. Then if you have time left over afterwards you can browse around the convention hall and find out more about other institutions that you might not already have considered.

Ask the advisers anything you like, such as: entry requirements; selection procedures; course structure and assessment; self-directed learning; costs; sponsorship opportunities; facilities and support; general questions about the institution; graduate prospects; contact details; or where to go for more information. Pick up as many relevant leaflets and prospectuses as you can. You may also want to attend seminars on the day about filling in application forms, writing personal statements or taking a gap year.

Connexions and UCAS provide a comprehensive pre-event support package , including the publication *Getting In, Getting On*, which is designed to enable you to get the best from a convention, and information on the UCAS website (www.ucas.com/students/exhibitions/howtoprepare). UCAS convention dates can also be found on its website (www.ucas.com/students/exhibitions/conventions).

Open days

Visiting a higher education institution allows you to see what it's like for yourself and make your own mind up. Universities hold departmental open days, open days for their individual colleges, and university-wide open days. Try to visit as many as your time and finances allow, although you will have to balance the number of visits against the disruption to your studies or employment.

Full listings of all British university open days can be found in the *Sixthformer's Guide 2008*, (published annually by Inspiring Futures Foundation), and *Open Days 2008* (published by UCAS). You can also check www.opendays.com. As dates may be announced late or subject to change, you should also contact institutions nearer the time you plan to visit to ensure that they will be proceeding as planned.

To get the very best out of the day, write a checklist of whatever's important to you. Take a notebook along with you and write down what you find out, as a reminder for when you get home. Observe your surroundings, reflect on your feelings and ask as many questions as you need to. Talk to students, and to academic and support staff.

Here is a sample checklist:

Course
- [ ] How interesting is the course?
- [ ] Any bits that look boring?
- [ ] Can I do well here?
- [ ] Entry requirements
- [ ] What current students say
- [ ] Careers a course could lead to
- [ ] Recognised by professional bodies?
- [ ] What is the department like?
- [ ] Who are the lecturers?
- [ ] How many students in each year?
- [ ] Course structure and flexibility
- [ ] Work experience or industrial placements
- [ ] Links with employers
- [ ] Teaching style
- [ ] Amount of independent study
- [ ] Facilities such as labs, equipment, lecture halls, etc.
- [ ] Key or transferable skills
- [ ] Chance to study abroad?

University
- [ ] What is the general atmosphere like?
- [ ] Type and size of campus
- [ ] Condition of buildings
- [ ] Where is my department?
- [ ] Does the campus feel friendly, safe?
- [ ] Is there anywhere to eat and drink?
- [ ] Access for disabled students
- [ ] What's the nearby town or city like?
- [ ] Extra-curricular learning opportunities
- [ ] Do I feel relaxed and at home here?

Transport
- [ ] Where are the transport links?
- [ ] How much does it cost?
- [ ] Will there be a lot of travel between campuses?
- [ ] Parking space, bike racks?

Support

- [ ] Student health services
- [ ] Employment centre
- [ ] Careers centre
- [ ] Student Union
- [ ] Welfare officers
- [ ] Disability officers
- [ ] Financial advisers

Facilities

- [ ] Library
- [ ] Lecture theatres and seminar rooms
- [ ] Computer labs
- [ ] Practical rooms
- [ ] Bars and clubs
- [ ] Sports fields, sports centres
- [ ] Launderette
- [ ] Shops

Accommodation

- [ ] How near to campus?
- [ ] Catered or self-catering?
- [ ] Safe area, security measures?
- [ ] Condition of buildings (inside and out)?
- [ ] How many sharing?
- [ ] How often are bills paid?
- [ ] What do students need to bring?
- [ ] What facilities are there?

Costs/financial

- [ ] Tuition fees
- [ ] Other fees
- [ ] Course equipment
- [ ] Field trips
- [ ] Cost of living
- [ ] Funding
- [ ] Sponsorship
- [ ] Bursaries
- [ ] Deposits
- [ ] Part-time jobs

Graduate prospects

- [ ] Percentage of graduates employed
- [ ] Drop-out rates
- [ ] Type of work graduates end up in
- [ ] Employers who visit the department/uni
- [ ] Further study options
- [ ] What students think of the careers centre
- [ ] Facilities at the careers centre

Social

- [ ] Clubs and societies
- [ ] Places to meet friends
- [ ] Practice rooms
- [ ] Nearby nightlife
- [ ] Cultural: theatre, art, music, cinema

It's up to you which of all those questions you ask, but as you can see, investigating a college or university can be quite a complex process.

> I picked Leeds firstly on how good the course was, but then I visited the open day and they really "sold it" to me.

Then there was the location: I wanted to move away from home but I'm from a big city and didn't want that to change really, or how much there is to do etc., and Leeds seemed perfect for me. Finally finding out other people's views that have been or are there helped, seeing their opinion of the uni . . . when they were all positive there was only one real choice for me. **'**

JAMIE HUGHES, AGE 17, STARTING MARKETING AT LEEDS METROPOLITAN UNIVERSITY

Pre-university taster courses

Another way of finding out what a university or college is really like is to participate in a 'taster' course there. These vary in length, from a one-day course to a longer summer school lasting a few weeks; these can be residential or non-residential. They range from sixth-form workshops to master-classes, study days and activity weeks. Subjects vary but are often scientific or technical.

It's an ideal way to show genuine interest in a course or subject, and it looks good on an application form. Taster courses can also give you the inside view of what a department's really like. To find out more, see the extensive taster course listings in the *Sixthformer's Guide 2008* (published by Inspiring Futures Foundation), or *Open Days 2008* (published by UCAS), or apply directly to institutions that you're interested in.

STUDYING OUTSIDE THE UK

An increasing number of UK students are deciding to study their degrees outside the UK. A full guide to this mode of study is outside the scope of this book, but some useful starting points are given below.

Republic of Ireland

The Central Applications Office (CAO) handles all applications to universities in the Republic of Ireland. The CAO website has an online application form, details of all courses and institutions, an application handbook, and details of university open days.

Central Applications Office
Tower House
Eglinton Street
Galway
Ireland
Tel: 00 353 (0)91 509 800
Fax: 00 353 (0)91 562 344
Website: www.cao.ie/index.php

UK Council for International Student Affairs

The UK Council for International Student Affairs (UKCISA) suggests that if you want to study a whole degree abroad, you will usually need to start researching possibilities 12–18 months in advance to allow sufficient time for making an application, completing any tests (including language tests) required, obtaining visas and finding funding.

UKCISA
9–17 St Albans Place
London N1 0NX
Advice Line: 020 7107 9922

For help and advice visit the webpages for UK students studying abroad at the UKCISA website (www.ukcosa.org.uk/student/ukstudent/index.php).

United Nations Educational Scientific and Cultural Organization

The United Nations Educational Scientific and Cultural Organization (UNESCO) 'Study Abroad' guide includes an online database of around 2,900 courses and scholarships available worldwide (www.unesco.org/ed_sa/cgi-bin/search/index.cgi). As well as basic course information, you can get an idea of what financial help may be available.

Braintrack University Index

Braintrack (www.braintrack.com) is the world's oldest and most complete university directory with over 8,300 links to higher education institutions in 194 countries. You can find universities by browsing countries or by advanced search.

SUMMARY: 10 TIPS FOR CHOOSING A UNIVERSITY

1. **There's no 'best' university**. There's only the best combination of course, subject, department, institution and overall environment *for you*.

2. **Be yourself**. Try not to be too influenced by peer pressure, family pressure, or where your friends are going. Be guided by your own interests, talents and preferences.

3. **See the big picture**. Don't be too easily swayed by one single book, website or person's opinion. Do plenty of reading and asking around to get a balanced overview.

4. **Make a shortlist**. Once you have an overview, start researching a few attractive institutions in much greater detail. You can begin to narrow your choices down from there.

5. **Check official information**. Make sure you are applying to a proper course at a recognised or listed institution. This is specially important if you are applying for an unusual or novel course, or considering a college you've never encountered before.

6. **Attend higher education conferences**. Get quality information from representatives from several institutions all under the same roof, and attend useful presentations.

7. **Collect prospectuses and course guides**. They will help you to decide where to apply to, how to write your applications, and perform well at interviews. Just remember they won't tell you about the downside of anything.

8. **Attend open days**. There's no substitute for visiting in person and making your own mind up. Make a checklist before you arrive, and take notes throughout the day.

9. **Keep asking questions**. Speak to careers advisers if you get stuck, and contact university admissions offices if information is unclear or incomplete.

10. **Consider a taster course**. See how a department functions on an everyday level, and have something good to add to an application form.

CHAPTER FOUR

THE APPLICATION

O nce you have chosen your courses and places to study, you can begin to prepare your application. The majority of applications are made through UCAS's standard application process. Applications that go through UCAS but are slightly different are those for medicine, dentistry and veterinary medicine and science, Route B art and design, and those for courses at Oxford or Cambridge.

Some teacher training and music courses are applied for through other bodies, and under certain circumstances, applications can also be made directly to colleges and universities themselves, such as applications to the Open University. These will be mentioned later, and let's start by concentrating on the most common UCAS route, which is also known as Route A.

OVERVIEW OF THE STANDARD UCAS APPLICATION PROCESS (ROUTE A)

Most applications for UK degree courses are made through a standard process run by UCAS. If everything goes well, the commonest route is:

1 You apply online via UCAS and are made an offer by your favourite university

2 You accept this as a firm offer (plus one insurance place)

3 You get your grades

4 You confirm your place.

However, if things don't go according to this simple plan, you also have the opportunity to apply through the UCAS Extra and Clearing processes. The Clearing process is outlined in the flow chart.

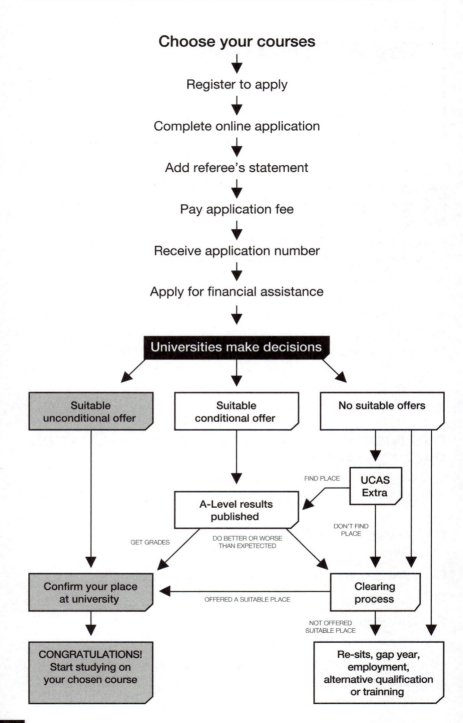

The process is slightly different if you are applying via UCAS for dentistry, medicine, veterinary medicine and science, and some art and design courses, or if you are hoping to enter Oxford or Cambridge. A few courses are also applied for outside the UCAS system. These variations will all be mentioned later in this chapter. For more information about UCAS Extra and details about Clearing, please see Chapters 7 and 8, respectively.

APPLICATION DEADLINE TIMETABLE

Once you have chosen your ideal courses, you must carefully check the application deadlines for each one, and if you're not certain then check directly with the individual universities themselves. The typical application year runs as follows:

DATE	EVENT
Start of September	Applications open for courses commencing the following September/October
Mid-October	Deadline for UCAS applications for medicine, dentistry, veterinary medicine and veterinary science
Mid-October	Deadline for UCAS applications for Oxford and Cambridge
Start of January	Applications open for Route B art and design courses
Mid-January	Deadline for most UCAS course applications (consideration not guaranteed after this date)
3rd week of March	'Route B' deadline for application for some art and design courses (although UCAS advises applying before the end of the 1st week of March if possible)
End of June	Last chance for UK and European Union students to apply for full-time courses through UCAS (consideration not guaranteed)
End of June	Last chance for guaranteed consideration for overseas students applying from outside the European Union to apply for full-time courses through UCAS (unless applying to Oxford or Cambridge, or for medicine, dentistry, veterinary science, veterinary medicine, or Route B art courses – in which case the specific UK deadlines apply)

Wherever possible, don't leave it until the last second to apply for courses may you as miss the deadlines. Vacancies on the most popular courses fill up quickly, and admissions tutors can start offering places as soon as they receive the applications. However, Darren Barker from UCAS says 'students don't have to rush to get their application in as long as they make the deadline. Admissions staff in universities and colleges use a wealth of experience built up from previous years when setting their entry standards and criteria, so can promise to consider equally all applications which are received on time.'

STANDARD UCAS APPLICATIONS

Almost all UCAS applications are now made online. The UCAS Apply system is a secure, web-based application system, which is available 24 hours a day. You fill in the application online when it suits you and it does not need to be completed all at once, so you are able to practise and take your time (you have the option to store and edit your details in Apply without submitting them). You can fill in the online form on any computer with internet access, and once you are happy with it and decide to submit it, the information goes immediately to UCAS. It's forwarded to your chosen universities and colleges within 48 hours.

Darren Barker from UCAS points out that while 'at present 99% of applications are done online, there are exceptional circumstances where we provide paper-based forms. These requests usually come from international applicants, although we do provide information regarding local online centres if people request paper forms. All the information about making a UCAS application is available on www.ucas.com and if students have signed up to the UCAS Card scheme, they will receive information in the form of e-bulletins and the *You Can* publication guiding them through the procedure. Tutors and advisers should also be well versed in the UCAS application process.'

If you're no longer in education you can apply as an independent applicant, and there will be slight differences in the way you fill the form in, which will be mentioned as we go along.

Here's the running order for completing the standard UCAS online form:

1 Register online at www.ucas.com

2 Log in to Apply

3 Check/fill in Personal details

4 Complete Additional information

5 Fill in Choices

6 Fill in Education

7 Complete Employment

8 Cut and paste in Personal statement

9 Add Reference (you or your referee)

10 Do final editing (if referee says it's needed)

11 Submit Form (you or your referee)

12 Pay UCAS

13 UCAS forwards applications to institutions

14 Use the online 'Track' system to follow progress.

IMPORTANT! MAKE SURE YOU DON'T LOSE . . .

- Your school or college buzzword (if there is one)
- The email address you gave to UCAS
- Your Track username/ID number and password
- Your UCAS application number.

CORINNE RILEY, AGE 18, FROM CHEADLE AND MARPLE SIXTH FORM COLLEGE

'UCAS Apply was great. I didn't actually use any of the help leaflets, and thought that the whole system was pretty quick and simple to complete, unlike a lot of other forms that get given out these days. All of my help came from my college's careers advisers who were always there if I wanted something checking, or to ask if I was doing everything right.

'I'm good with passwords and usernames, so I never lost them, I was never locked out of the system, and when I sent my application to my college for my referee to *add comments, it went straight there. I think it's a better system than having to apply through the post anyway!'*

FILLING IN THE UCAS APPLICATION FORM

The Apply system is fairly simple to use, with help text available throughout to assist you to complete each section. There is also detailed advice on the UCAS website (www.ucas.com), and if you still can't find what you're looking for, you can contact the UCAS Customer Service Unit on 0871 468 0468 to speak to an adviser. If you are at school or college, your tutors should also be able to explain things and troubleshoot many problems.

The online system is designed for viewing using a browser such as Internet Explorer, but there are no technical issues with other browsers such as Firefox. Most users have no technical problems at all, but there are two online guides that can help you cope with the occasional glitch:

- www.ucas.com/advisers/apply/techissues/hardwareandinternetsettings
- www.ucas.com/advisers/apply/techissues/knownissues/

ONLINE CENTRES

If you don't have access to a personal computer with an internet connection, and you're fighting for computer time at college or school, there is an alternative option. Over 900 online centres are participating in a scheme with UCAS and will allow you to use their computers for free. They will not be able to offer you any support or advice specific to the application, but you will be able to view the UCAS website, set up an account, and use Apply and Track.

ALEX CLAYTON, AGE 18, OSSETT SIXTH FORM, WAKEFIELD

'I found getting into Apply was all fine. It didn't take me too much time at all to complete the form. It was getting it through my school system that took the longest time! I didn't use a leaflet, nor did I need to - it was all very obvious. I didn't really have any problems at all, except that it took a bit of time to find all the music qualifications and getting the orders right for my exams. Oh, it WAS a little

confusing as to how I entered my AS levels and A levels, whether we had to enter both or not etc. . . . The only thing I could be picky about is that the form kept coming back to me with "errors" from my form tutor, although neither of us could find them. That was a bit annoying but it got sorted out. Apart from that it made total sense, was not difficult at all, and for the most part it was reliable! The odd server downtime interrupted my application and meant I lost any unsaved info, but otherwise it was comprehensive and easy to use.'

Getting started: registration

You have to register before you can use Apply. Even at this early stage, take great care over your spelling and use of upper and lower case letters. University staff will be reading some of what you type in here, so make it look like a professional document from the start, rather than a text message to your best mate.

Darren Barker says 'If you're registering through your school, college or careers organisation you need their "buzzword", which will be given to you by your tutor or careers adviser. When you enter this buzzword during the registration process, it links your application to your school so that your tutor can write your reference.' Buzzwords are case sensitive so type with care. Don't forget to use the buzzword, as without it your tutor or year head won't be able to provide you with a reference. If you do forget it, you'll have to ask your college or school to contact UCAS so that they can change your application over to the right system. You don't need a buzzword if you are applying independently.

To register, go to www.ucas.com and click 'Apply', then click 'Student login' for your chosen year of entry. Click 'Register', read the terms and conditions, then click 'Next'.

If you're applying via your school or college, click on the school or college, and then type the buzzword into the box and click 'Next'. You will be taken to a screen saying you are at a particular school or college, and if it's correct, click 'Yes' to be taken to a drop-down list to select your tutor. Then click 'Next' to continue to the contact details stage. If you are applying independently, skip the part where you click on a school or college, and go straight to the contact details.

You will arrive at a screen where you fill in your name and date of birth – make sure that the 'UK' button is selected if you're applying from the UK. Then type in your postcode and full address, telephone number(s) and email address and click 'Next'. Use an email address that you check regularly and won't forget the password for, but don't pick one like vodkaredbull@wasted.net or iM2Sexxi@facebookedyamum. com. The next screen will ask you to check the details you have entered so far. Go back and edit even the tiniest mistake. Once you're happy, click on 'Next'.

You will then be given your unique Apply username, and asked to choose a password. Write down both of them and keep them somewhere very safe. And that's it – you've registered.

You can now decide whether to go straight on and continue with the rest of the application, or come back to it later.

If you do decide to come back to the application after taking a break, go to www.ucas.com and click on 'Apply', then 'Student login', and type in your registration username and password. If you get it wrong too many times you will get locked out of the system. If you're confused at any point, you can use the 'How to use Apply' help information.

Click on any section title to open it (you can complete them in any order) and add to it. You can save what you have done so far if you need to take a break at any time. Once you have completed a section to your satisfaction, click the 'Section finished' button and go on to the next one.

Personal details ('About you')

Your name, title, home address, phone number(s), date of birth and email will be on this part of the form already – check that they're all correct. You will then be asked to fill in your country of birth, your nationality, your residential status, and your student support codes and arrangements. Take care when entering student support codes and other financial data, as one common mistake is saying you are privately funded when you aren't (being completely privately funded is relatively uncommon, and is not about having a high parental income or applying for student loans). Next, you'll be asked about special needs: these include dyslexia, disabilities and chronic health conditions such as diabetes and epilepsy.

DAVID FINE, AGE 19, STUDYING MUSIC AND CREATIVE WRITING AT BATH SPA UNIVERSITY

'The only tricky parts are the financial bits, whether the funding's from an LEA [local education authority] or private source, etc. The UCAS leaflet's good too, particularly on explaining the Track process and the different combinations of choices. The whole application takes a while, but it's all worth it - it's just a long application that needs care, rather than being long through over-complication.

'Doing everything online is so much easier. It can be accessed from anywhere, saved and come back to, clearer (no handwriting issues), it disables questions if you've said something in a previous question that makes another no longer relevant. The automatic nature of the system makes it a pretty easy system to have to deal with.

'If I had anything bad to say about it at all, it's the Track system. It'd be nice if it'd email more regularly, rather than the two updates at 12pm and 5pm. I had an embarrassing call this year where I called the uni to ask why they'd missed the deadline they'd told me beforehand - they said they'd actually already updated it a few hours previously, but I couldn't actually access Track for a few more hours. I wanted to tell everyone I had my place, but couldn't actually confirm it!'

Additional information

This is for UK applicants only, and you can expect to be asked about your non-examination-based activities, plus some monitoring information that remains with UCAS and is not passed on to the universities, including your ethnic origin and the occupation of your highest earning parent.

Choices

Usually you can make up to five choices, but you can have only one if you like. Applying for more than one course at the same university counts as more than one choice.

Place each choice on a separate line, either typing the name in or using the UCAS course codes. Make sure you have all the course codes correctly entered. Once you've saved them, the software rearranges everything alphabetically, regardless of the order in which they were added.

None of the universities you apply to will be told about which other institutions you've applied to, so don't worry that this will somehow count against you. However, if you apply for two or more different courses at the same university or college, that institution will know that you have applied for more than one place with them.

PLANNING A DEFERRAL?

The usual application deadlines for the current year will still apply to you, and if you accept a place for the following year you cannot then reapply for other places during the following year unless you withdraw your original application. If you are going to defer, you must fill in the correct box on the online application to make it official.

Applying a year ahead is by far the easiest thing to do if you're still at school or college and planning a gap year. You'll be on site and able to communicate with tutors and referees more easily, and there should be plenty of help during the application process if you get stuck. If you leave it until the following academic year you might not get this level of support, and it can be hard to make arrangements if you are working or travelling overseas. To read more about gap year and deferral, see Chapter 1.

You may need to add in some extra course-specific information (a code or codes) for certain courses. Check the UCAS website for every course you choose to see whether there's anything in the 'Details required to fill in your UCAS form' section.

There will also be some more boxes to fill in or leave blank for each separate course:

- One box asks about whether if you wish to live in your present home while you are at university.
- 'Defer entry' (if you're applying now, but planning to take a year off before starting your studies, you need to remind the college or university of your intentions).
- 'Point of entry' (leave blank unless you want to apply for entry into the second year at a university in Scotland).

Be certain that you have filled these boxes correctly for every single course before you mark the section as complete.

At the end of this section, applicants who are not still at school will be asked about previous applications through UCAS. You will then be asked whether you want to apply for Route B art and design courses – the answer will be 'No' for most applicants, but there's more about Route B later in this chapter if your answer is 'Yes'.

Education

First you need to fill in the places where you have studied. If you haven't finished school yet, fill in the date you started, and leave the 'date of leaving' box blank. Then enter all your qualifications by clicking on the correct category (GCSE/GCE, AS level, A level, other, etc.), and making sure you enter the exact title of the subject, the date taken (if completed), and the right examination board. The summary screen will list your qualifications. If you haven't taken the exams yet, they will be highlighted as being without final grades. Universities base their offers on your qualifications, so make sure it's correct – and remember, they can check up on it.

TIM MAHY, AGE 26, CURRENTLY A CONTRACT ACCOUNTANT WORKING IN GUERNSEY

'I found Apply very easy to use. I just went on, looked at what I needed to input, collated the info and entered it. Easy as pie! Reliable and simple. I went in and made a couple of amendments, no problems whatsoever. The only problem I had was that there was no area to enter non-standard educational information. I'm a mature student and the whole form is essentially aimed at the students doing A levels and equivalent qualifications, but quite a proportion of students have non-standard entrance qualifications. I've got accountancy qualifications and used these for my entrance as they are degree and masters level exams, proving that I am able to study at high levels. The only place I could mention these was in my personal statement. A separate area for these types of qualifications, in my opinion, would be more appropriate.'

Employment

This section is for any paid work you have done, including full-time, part-time and holiday jobs. Remember to put the name of the company down, and not the name of your manager. You shouldn't include volunteer work or unpaid work experience in this section. If you have a long employment history you can also send your full work history directly to the colleges and universities you're applying to after you've filled in everything else on the form. If you haven't had a job before, don't worry. Just leave the section blank, then mark it as complete and carry on with the rest of the application.

Personal statement

The personal statement is usually prepared in a separate word processing document, then cut and pasted into the online Apply form.

This section is the only part of the form where applicants get to write anything substantial in their own words. It's an excellent opportunity to explain why your chosen course interests you and the reasons you think you'd make a good candidate. On courses where there's intense competition for spaces, this can make or break your application. In fact, it's so important to get it right that the whole of Chapter 5 of this guide is devoted to it – please flip through to find out more.

Some universities no longer interview many of their applicants, so your personal statement can strongly influence whether you're made an offer or not. Also, at universities and colleges that do hold interviews, many interview questions concentrate on aspects of the personal statement, so it's essential to be both interesting and honest in your writing.

The reference

Remember to keep your referee informed of your progress to give them plenty of time to prepare their reference.

Darren Barker from UCAS ran us through the responsibilities of applicants and referees. 'If an applicant is at school or college or has recently left, then they should get the head teacher, principal or an appropriate teacher to write the reference. Once an applicant has completed their online application, they then send it to their referee, who will then check through it and write their reference. They will then send it to UCAS. Applicants applying through a school or college don't have access to the reference.

'If an applicant is applying as an individual, they should ask a responsible person who knows them well enough to provide their reference. This could be an employer, training officer, careers adviser, a teacher on a recent relevant further education course, or a senior colleague in employment or voluntary work. It is their responsibility to obtain the reference and add it to their online application before sending the application to UCAS.'

You will need to cut and paste their reference into the form.

Sending off the application

Once you have completed all the sections of the form that you need to, check and edit it until you're happy, then print out some paper copies of the form to keep.

As mentioned above, school or college applicants need to send the application to their referee, who might come back to them for some more editing, and who will then forward it to UCAS. You will be asked to agree to a declaration. Read it carefully before ticking the box and clicking 'I agree'.

Independent applicants forward the form to UCAS themselves by agreeing to the declaration, then moving on to arrange payment.

Payment

If you're applying through your school, college or centre, your organisation will let you know how they want you to pay. It will be either by credit or debit card online via the Apply system, or by paying the school or other registered centre who will then pay UCAS on your behalf. If applying as an individual, you will need to make the payment via the Apply system using a credit or debit card. The card need not be in your own name, but you will require the consent of the cardholder. If you're applying for more than one course, it costs £15 to use the UCAS Apply service (or £5 if you are only applying for one course).

Once you have completed your application and sent it, you will get a message saying that the application has been sent to UCAS (or it will be sent to your referee if you're applying through a school, college or other organisation).

Congratulations! Your application is now on its way. Good luck.

Monitoring your progress

Once the application has been processed, you will be sent a welcome letter by UCAS with details about how to use the online Track function. You will be able to follow the progress of your application, and update your address details if they've changed, using Track. For all options you will need to know your original application number and password.

As each university or college processed your application, UCAS updates the details on Track. You can check online regularly, or sign up to be alerted by email or a text message when these changes are made. Each university has its own process for dealing with admissions. You may be asked to attend for interviews or tests (see Chapter 6), or you may simply receive offers or rejections (see Chapter 7). Universities should aim to send all decisions to applicants by the end of March, so long as the application was received before the middle of January (with the exception of Route B). In practice, some universities do not reply until the start of the second week of May, and if they're later than this with their reply, it becomes a rejection by default.

D, ABOUT TO START MEDIA PRODUCTION AT THE ATRIUM AT THE UNIVERSITY OF GLAMORGAN

'I really REALLY ... didn't like Apply if I'm honest! I think its very confusing (maybe that's just me but hey) and the layout of the website could be improved. It's not bad in my opinion but it could be clearer. It's relatively quick, after having to spend ages cutting out bits of my personal statement to make it fit. I had my application sent back because although I actually put in module titles where it told me to, four people at the student services at my college had to try and get their head around my application because the website didn't make things clear enough. Though I didn't lose any of my usernames or passwords I kept getting locked out for some reason. Then I entered the same details a few days later and it was fine.

'No complaints with the correspondence though. I like that they send you emails when your application changes so you know when you have an offer or not. The email notifications were really useful and it's useful having everything online so there's no pieces of paper to lose. It is easy to edit, but I think a "restore to saved draft" option would be useful in case you accidentally close it before saving changes.'

☑ **TIP**

Apply for financial help – student grants and student loans – as soon as you've made your applications. You don't need to wait for the offer of a course.

CHANGING YOUR UCAS APPLICATION

If your home address, phone number or email address change, you should let UCAS know immediately. This can be done on Track or by contacting customer services (see below).

Sometimes applicants have a change of heart about their choice of one or more of their universities or colleges. If that happens to you, you can change your university or college choices on Track, but only if you do so within 14 days of receiving your welcome letter. After 14 days you cannot usually change them, unless there are special circumstances, and your referee writes to UCAS to explain them.

If you're happy with your choice of institution, but have changed your mind about your course, deferral, or the point of entry, you must write to the institution directly, which will then inform UCAS of their decision and the results will be posted on Track.

UCAS strongly recommends that you ask somebody to check through your application before it is submitted to make sure that there are no errors in the form. If an error is found after submitting a form there are ways in which it can be rectified. You should contact UCAS on 0871 468 0 468, and you will be given help to follow the correct procedure.

For information about withdrawing your UCAS application, please refer to Chapter 7. This is not a decision to be taken lightly, and it means you cannot enter Clearing.

MEDICINE, DENTISTRY, VETERINARY MEDICINE, VETERINARY SCIENCE

You can apply to these courses using the standard UCAS service, with one exception. Rather than the standard maximum of five choices, if you apply for one of the above subjects you can only make up to four choices within that specific subject. The remaining space (or spaces) on your application can be used as an insurance choice and can be for any other subject. Note the early closing date of mid-October for these applications.

To accompany your application you may be asked to provide the results of entry tests by a set date (see Chapter 6 for details) and/or proof that you have been vaccinated against the hepatitis B virus.

APPLYING FOR OXFORD OR CAMBRIDGE

You can apply to only one course at either Oxford University or the University of Cambridge, and you can't apply to both institutions at the same time (unless you already have a degree). This leaves you with up to four choices for courses at other universities. You will also be required to fill in an additional application form if you want to apply to Oxford, which can be obtained from the university or via some schools and colleges. The mid-October UCAS application deadline also applies.

ART AND DESIGN – ROUTE A AND ROUTE B

If you're applying for art and design courses you can apply for some through the standard UCAS route (Route A) and others via Route B. You may apply via Route A only, Route B only, or through Route A and Route B at the same time.

UCAS representative Darren Barker explains that

'Route B allows time for applicants studying a Diploma in Foundation Studies (Art and Design) to identify their specialisation and prepare their portfolio, although anyone can apply for a Route B course.

'For Route B courses, you can list up to three choices in preference order. UCAS must receive applications between September and the following 24 March, but we recommend that you apply by 7 March to avoid the last-minute rush. You will be asked to indicate your first choice, second choice and third choice.

'We will send your application to your first choice, which will decide whether to invite you for an interview and then whether to make you an offer. If you decide to accept the offer, we will cancel your other choices. If you turn down the offer, or you do not receive an offer, we will send your application to your second choice, and so on. We will start sending Route B applications to first choice universities and colleges from 12 February. If we receive your application after this date, we will send it to your first choice as soon as we have processed it.

'When applying to a Route B course their personal statement and the presentation and content of their portfolio allows students to showcase their talents and extra curricular activities.'

NON-UCAS APPLICATIONS

While almost all undergraduate courses in the UK are now applied for via UCAS, there are a few exceptions, including January entry, music schools and some forms of teacher training.

January entry

If you're applying for January entry to some courses, you may have to apply to the university or college directly, although most courses with these start dates, such as nursing degrees and diplomas, are now applied to using the standard UCAS procedure. If you're applying for January entry, don't forget to allow the institution enough time to consider your application.

CUKAS

CUKAS handles applications to practice-based music courses at the following UK conservatoires:

- Birmingham Conservatoire
- Leeds College of Music
- Royal College of Music
- Royal Northern College of Music
- Royal Scottish Academy of Music and Drama
- Royal Welsh College of Music and Drama
- Trinity College of Music.

The applications are made via a service supported by UCAS, so they are uploaded using Apply and followed using Track. Applications open in early

July for admission the following year, and should ideally be submitted by the start of October. Auditions may begin as early as mid-October. For more details on dates for applying, auditions, decisions and replying, phone CUCAS on 0871 468 0470 or visit www.cukas.ac.uk/dates.html.

Teacher training

There are several routes into teacher training, including some applications made through UCAS. If you are applying for employment-based Initial Teacher Training you need to apply through your nearest employment-based Initial Teacher Training (EBITT) provider. To find out where they are, contact the Training and Development Agency for Schools on its teaching information line (0845 600 0991) or via its website (www.tda.gov.uk/partners/recruiting/ebr/drbs/ebittcontacts.aspx).

For applications for entry to Postgraduate and Professional Graduate Certificate in Education (PGCE) and Professional Graduate Diploma in Education (PGDE) courses you need to use the Graduate Teacher Training Registry (GTTR). GTTR acts on behalf of Initial Teacher Training (ITT) providers, which offer teacher training in England and Wales, and all Scottish higher education institutions (except the University of Paisley, to which you apply directly). GTTR applications are made online via its website, and followed using Track. For more information contact the customer service unit on 0871 468 0469 from within the UK or +44 871 468 0469 if you are calling from outside the UK, or look up details on its website (www.gttr.ac.uk/how/index.html).

APPLYING FOR PART-TIME AND FLEXIBLE LEARNING

If you have decided to start a part-time or flexible learning course rather than a full-time undergraduate course, you should apply directly to the institution. These details can be found on the Hotcourses website (www.hotcourses.com), on the www.direct.gov.uk course database powered by Learndirect, and in the prospectuses of individual higher education providers. For the Open University, you can register online (www.open.ac.uk) or by phone (0845 300 6090).

KATE IS STUDYING BA LINGUISTICS AND LANGUAGES PART-TIME AT BIRKBECK AS A MATURE STUDENT

'When I moved to London, I took an evening class in Spanish, primarily to make new friends and because I wanted the challenge of learning a new language. Several years later, I took six months off to travel in South America, and when I returned looked for a class where I could keep up with my Spanish and learn more about linguistics. At this time, I noticed a couple of my friends were doing post-grad or diploma courses at Birkbeck University and seemed to be having a really good time there. I went to their website and was very impressed by the choice of courses on offer.

'I originally went to an open evening and was told that Linguistics was only offered as a joint honour with a language – Spanish was my best language at that time but because it was mainly spoken (rather than written) they recommended I do an access course to get up to speed. I also did this through Birkbeck (you had to complete a written assessment) and at the end of the year the college was very keen for students to continue onto a degree course. Because I'd passed my Spanish course, I was automatically accepted onto that part of the degree and I was required to write a short essay for the Linguistics aspect. I also had interviews for both parts of the course and was told during the Linguistics interview that I'd been accepted on the course. I didn't apply anywhere else as I could only study part-time due to work commitments.

'The best thing about the degree has been learning to think again. It's felt incredibly liberating and exciting to sit down and research a subject and develop my own ideas and theories about it. Because it was a subject that I was always interested in, it's been great to find out more about it and also to discover previously unknown topics, like the psychology aspect of the course, which I didn't expect to enjoy so much. Obviously the lack of time can be hard; a four-year commitment of at least two nights a week, plus more for home studying and having to pass upon invitations to stay in to do homework can be somewhat wearing. I think I've been most surprised by how much I've enjoyed it and how quickly it's going.'

SUMMARY BOX: TOP TIPS FOR APPLICATIONS

1. **Keep it smart**. Remember that the applications tutors will be able to see everything you have entered, so use correct grammar, not text-speak, and put capital letters in the right places.

2. **Know the deadlines**. Give yourself plenty of time to apply so that you can get your personal statement looking perfect and the rest of your application form properly filled in with all the right information.

3. **Respect the referee**. You also need to give your referee enough time to write a proper personal reference for you. It's hard for them to do that if you spring it on them at the eleventh hour, so be polite, keep them informed of your progress and let them know when you'll be needing their input.

4. **Don't rush it**. You can save whatever you're working on in Apply and come back to it whenever you feel like it. There's no need to feel pressured into rushing the whole thing through in one go.

5. **Extra, extra – read all about it**. If you apply to certain courses, you may have to enter additional codes into the system to complete the application. Check on the UCAS website for all the details for each course you're applying to.

6. **The personal statement's different**. It's the only part of the form where you can put things into your own words and stand out from the crowd. Take your time over it, and write the draft using a word processing program.

7. **Slightly different**. Note that UCAS applications for medicine, dentistry, veterinary medicine and science, Oxford and Cambridge, and Route B art and design courses have variations in the way you apply.

8. **You're not alone**. If you get stuck there are UCAS leaflets, website help and troubleshooting pages, and a customer service line. You may also get help from your school or college tutors and careers advisers.

9. **Keep Track of it all**. You can use the UCAS online Track function to follow your progress and to reply to offers. It can be set up to send you emails or text messages. All you need is your Track username and password, and your application number.

10. **Slightly different again**. Although almost all applications for undergraduate courses in the UK are made via UCAS, conservatoires, some teaching courses and part-time courses are applied to by different routes – check with each institution you're considering to find out how and when to apply.

CHAPTER FIVE
ADVICE FOR THE UCAS PERSONAL STATEMENT

The personal statement section of the UCAS form is your chance to shine. It's likely to be your best opportunity to impress admissions tutors and stand out from the rest of the competition, so it's worth making the effort to make it as well written and informative as possible. Many students find this part of the application process daunting, but if you take the time to research and prepare properly, you should end up with a statement that shows you in your best light.

It's often the first time that students have been asked to write about and 'sell' themselves, and their dreams and aspirations, so naturally it might feel a little difficult getting started. However, it's also your chance to review the decisions that you've made so far, to reflect on what's really important to you, and consider your strengths and weaknesses.

> ❝ I know some people didn't like the personal statement limit, but that's nothing to do with the online system really. Presumably that's just because admissions tutors don't want to read a novel by each applicant, they want a succinct summary. I'm not saying that doing that was easy, but I can't see how they could avoid setting a word limit. ❞
> **JAMES HEGGIE, AGE 21, STUDYING MEDICINE AT THE UNIVERSITY OF BIRMINGHAM**

Here's a step-by-step guide on how to get the most out of the personal statement:

1. Think about what admissions tutors are looking for
2. Research your courses properly

3 Spend plenty of time preparing

4 Write a careful first draft

5 Be ready to rewrite it several times

6 Double check everything

7 Follow UCAS's uploading instructions

8 Pass the application on to your referee in good time

9 Refer back to statement for interviews, Clearing, UCAS Extra, etc.

Beth Hayes, UCAS's website editor, explains why the personal statement is such a crucial part of the application form: 'A personal statement allows students the chance to stand out of the crowd by telling an institution why they should choose them over someone else with the same grades. It can be one of the most important parts of the application process, so time and care should be taken when filling in this section. It could be the basis for an interview, so students should be prepared to answer questions on it. A student may want to list extra-curricular activities, what career they are working toward and how they will benefit from the degree course that they want to study. They should try to link their hobbies and interests to the skills/experience required for the course.'

WHAT DO ADMISSIONS STAFF WANT TO KNOW?
Here are some questions from admissions staff at the University of Leicester that a good personal statement should answer.

- What makes you unique, special or impressive?
- What interests you about the course for which you are applying?
- How did you learn about this course/field of work?
- What is your relevant work experience?
- What are your career goals?
- What skills do you have (and can you back your claims up)?
- What personal characteristics do you possess (and can you provide evidence)?
- What responsibilities have you undertaken?
- What difficulties have you overcome?

MAKING YOUR STATEMENT COUNT

The purpose of writing the personal statement is to make you appealing to one particular target audience: admissions tutors at your chosen institutions. To make it as effective as possible, you should put yourself in their shoes when you're creating the text, and think about what they'd like to learn about you that isn't mentioned elsewhere on the UCAS form.

Tutors want to know that you're genuinely interested in your chosen course, that you understand what the course involves, and that you're capable of doing well academically. You need to show them that you're enthusiastic, motivated and dedicated, and ideally you need to demonstrate that the subject is part of your plans for the future after you've graduated. Aside from the course, they will also want to see some evidence that you'll adjust to a new environment, thrive at college or university, and make a positive contribution to the institution.

The best students show commitment, independence and maturity, and that they have enquiring minds and can think for themselves. Tutors need to know what you are like as a person, and are most likely to select applicants they see as 'well-rounded individuals'. High grades are not enough; they want you to have some 'get up and go', and a life away from your studies as well.

The people who will be reading your personal statement are busy individuals, and each one of them will have their own idea of what's appealing. It's important to understand that there's no accounting for their personal taste, and there's no set or 'perfect' way to craft your statement that can give you 100% assurance of success. All you can do is be true to yourself, prepare it carefully using the pointers in this chapter and give it your best shot.

JANNINE, FIRST-YEAR CRIMINOLOGY STUDENT AT UNIVERSITY OF THE WEST OF ENGLAND, BRISTOL

'I looked at other people's personal statements first to get an idea, it's really hard to start writing one from scratch. I also copied relevant pieces from my CV. All our personal statements had to be checked by a member of staff preferably in the area of the subject you were applying for at uni before sending them off. They would then be checked again once uploaded onto UCAS by our assigned referee before they would officially send it off to UCAS. Trying to say something positive about yourself can be hard . . . trying to sell all your best parts and not be negative at all. It's hard getting the first few starting lines down, after that it's OK. I also wrote loads of versions before my final one. I'm still not entirely happy with my statement looking back on it, but I got my place at uni so I'm happy! Once uploaded and sent off there's nothing you can do really except go with the flow.

'My opening paragraph is: "I am interested in studying Criminology at degree level as I would like to further my knowledge, particularly in relation to crime and how society deals with crime, and the psychological aspect of what makes people commit crimes. I have not decided on a definite career path at the moment, but have taken an interest in maybe working for the police force through criminology."

'My closing paragraph is: "I would really enjoy studying criminology, as it fits in with much of my own personal interests, and I am always willing to learn new things and to build on my existing knowledge in order to form new ideas and opinions."'

RESEARCH

The best place to start is by going back through each of the courses you've decided to apply for. Read the prospectuses and any other related information

WHAT ABOUT COMMERCIAL COMPANIES?

There are several companies out there that will write or 'improve' your personal statement for you for a fee. Unfortunately, not all of them are reputable, and you might not end up with an original, high-quality statement. While it's understandable that people might be keen to create the best personal statement that they can, there's no guarantee that buying one will ensure admission. Also, the person who knows you best is you – that's why it's called the 'personal statement' in the first place – so other people, especially if they're strangers, are probably not that well-suited to writing yours. Remember, at the end of your UCAS application you need to agree to a declaration that states the contents are complete, accurate and all your own work.

very carefully; course content and structure are extremely important, as we'll see later. If you're lucky, the websites of the institutions you're applying to may contain specific information about personal statements, and what they're expecting from one. Gather as much information as you can together, so it's all in one place, and check the admissions criteria.

Think hard about what attracts you to these particular courses, especially if they are subjects that you haven't formally studied yet. Look back at what led up to you becoming interested in your subject, and think about ways to show that you'd be a good candidate to study it at a higher level. If you have chosen more than one subject to apply for, ask yourself whether there's one reason in particular why they all appeal, and think very carefully about the things that these diverse courses have in common.

PREPARATION

It helps to make plenty of background notes before you start writing the personal statement properly. If certain phrases stand out in course prospectuses or on departmental websites, write them down. The same goes for positive comments that people have made about you – in school reports, references for part-time or full-time jobs, and so on. Think about what the course can do for you, and what you can bring to the course and the college or university.

Try covering as many of the points as you can in the checklists given below, but don't worry if you don't have an answer for everything on each list – you're not expected to have every single qualification or piece of experience.

Think deeper about the course you have applied for, and write down:

- Reasons why the course appeals to you.
- Anything you have studied that's related, and how it has led to your interest in the subject.
- What knowledge you already have about the subject, and how you have developed it.
- Elements of the course you're especially interested in – be prepared to go into detail here.

- Personal experiences that have led to your decision to study the subject.
- How you expect course theory to be put into practice.
- Why the subject is important in the modern world, or everyday life.
- Relevant work experience or placements.
- Language skills or previous travel that might be useful for your course.
- Other skills, knowledge or experience you have that might help on the course, such as design, model making, mentoring, first aid training, etc.

Consider as many of the items as you can in the following academic checklist:

- Your academic experience so far (no need to go into detail if you have already put this information elsewhere on your UCAS application).
- Any special topics you have already studied that have caught your attention, and why they interest you.
- Relevant modules, practical work or projects that were especially enjoyable, or highlight any of your knowledge or talents.
- Extra work you have done around the subject, including additional reading and independent research, entering competitions, or having something published or broadcast.
- Attending conferences or workshops.
- Prizes you have been awarded.
- Being part of a programme for gifted students or attending master classes.
- Attending summer schools or access courses.
- Related key skills, including communication, IT, etc.
- Sponsorships or placements you have applied for, or already been awarded.
- Courses etc. you have studied that are not accredited or mentioned elsewhere in the UCAS application.
- Memberships or subscriptions.
- Evidence that your language skills are good enough to study at university level, if your first language isn't English.

Next, consider your hopes for the future:

- Your main career goal, or what you hope to do after the course.
- Other related career goals, and possible specialism at a later date.
- How you think this course will help you reach your career goals.
- What you hope to get out of your time at university.

Lastly, think about what you are like as a person:

- Hobbies and interests.
- Sports or fitness, other leisure activities.
- Full-time or part-time jobs.
- Positions of responsibility held at work, in school or college, or in your spare time.
- Schemes you are part of, such as Millennium Volunteers, Duke of Edinburgh's Award Scheme, Youth Enterprise Scheme, Award Scheme Development and Accreditation Network (ASDAN) Awards, mentoring, sports leadership, Prince's Trust, local awards and so on.
- Voluntary work, community projects or fundraising.
- Teams or societies you are part of.
- Prizes you have won at the local, county or national level.
- Any non-academic achievements.
- Skills you have gained from your experiences, such as time management, the ability to work in a team or supervise, dealing with difficult people, working under pressure or to deadlines, being analytical, reasoning and communicating, etc.
- Personal qualities: enthusiasm, reliability, independence, trustworthiness, creativity, etc.
- Major events in your life that have strongly affected you.
- Plans for a gap year, if you intend to take one, and how this might relate to your course.

❝The software was quite easy to use, at least I didn't have any problems with it and didn't need to use the leaflet. I would agree with some other people that there should be a separate section for non-academic qualifications as they do take up a lot of space in the personal statement (which in itself is quite hard to condense – 18 odd years in 4,000 characters). **,**

CHARLOTTE BRYAN, AGE 18, FROM HIGH STORRS SCHOOL, SHEFFIELD

Reading what other people have written

Once you have some of your background facts, ideas and phrases collected together, you can begin to draw inspiration from personal statements that other students have had success with. Collect several together and compare them. Where possible, look at applications for the subjects that interest you most. You can find examples on the internet, in books, or perhaps from teachers, tutors or careers officers. Study the contents and flow of the text, the running order of the paragraphs, the length and structure of sentences, and the different writing styles and vocabulary of previous students. This should give you a rough idea of what's more likely to be successful. While this process should really inform and inspire you, don't be tempted to copy anything word for word – not even half a sentence. Your statement has to be original: yours, and yours alone.

WRITING THE FIRST DRAFT

Before you start writing the text of your statement, check with UCAS to make sure you know exactly how the process works, and what's expected of you. There are basic instructions and a question and answer section on the website (www.ucas.com), and there's a helpline to call if you get stuck or have software problems (0871 468 0468). Applicants also receive UCAS booklets, and if you're at school or college your tutors may have created some reference materials of their own to help you.

It's recommended that you type into a word processing document to begin with, and not the actual online UCAS form. This is because you should expect to make lots of changes to the statement before it's finally ready. Although it's possible to save and edit your statement online with UCAS without sending it off, you could accidentally submit it before it's ready and after that point you will not be able to make changes to it. It's much better to work on different versions in, for example, Microsoft Word™, and then cut and paste the final version into the online form when you're happy with everything.

You can write up to 4,000 characters (this includes spaces and punctuation), or 47 lines of text. On average this works out at about 600 words, so you can use that as a rough idea when you're writing your initial draft.

Should you fill all the available space? Well, it's a definite case of quality being more important than quantity, and it's best not to pad it out with waffle or comments that are not interesting or relevant. However, it's also an opportunity to make a great case for yourself, so if you can fill out the whole section persuasively and with some flair then you should try to do so. In other words, say what you need to say and then stop, but it's best if you have a lot of useful things to say.

How can the same statement suit the different places you have applied to?

Remember that, with very few exceptions, the same statement goes out to all your chosen universities and colleges, so you need to be careful what you write to avoid alienating some of them. According to Beth Hayes from UCAS, students 'can only do one personal statement, which will be sent to all the institutions that they apply to (unless applying for Route A courses first, then adding Route B choices to their application later). The likelihood is that applicants will be applying to similar courses, so their personal statement should be tailored towards the type of courses they have applied to. If they apply to more then one course, it's a good idea to focus on the skills and experience required for each course, rather than the subjects. If applicants apply through Extra or Clearing for a different course to their original choices, they should contact the new university or college and ask if they would consider a new personal statement. They can then send a new statement direct to the university or college.'

If you're applying for five similar courses, each at different institutions, the individual universities and colleges will not know who else you've applied to because UCAS doesn't tell them. Keep it that way. Don't mention any of them by name in your personal statement as not only will you put off the ones you *don't* name, you might also look naïve or desperate to the ones you *do* name. Similarly, don't mention course specifics (modules, topics, practical work, work experience, etc.) if they are included on some of the courses but not others. It will make admissions tutors think that you don't know much about their course, or that you're not really interested in it, if you get the facts wrong. Only mention items that all the courses have in common.

It gets much trickier if you have decided to apply for courses that are not all similar. You have to be even more careful here so that you don't slip up and give the game away. You might need to talk in more general terms about the subjects without naming them outright, and concentrate on what you have gained overall from your academic and personal experiences. Generally speaking though, the more competition there is for places on a particular course, the less vague you should be if you want to get in. For example, when applying for dual honours degrees, be aware that some admissions tutors will not look kindly on you if you fail to mention both components of the degree. Take plenty of time when wording your statement if you're looking at a number of dual honours degrees which don't have similar titles. Failing that, you might have to go with wording that's tailored to fit your top few choices, but that might appear less specific to tutors at your less favoured institutions. Or you might decide to be open about it, and explain clearly why you have applied to different courses.

If none of your chosen courses have much in common, consider revisiting the choices you have made, especially if your personal statement is looking hopelessly vague. It could be worth going back a few steps and rethinking what you want to study, and coming back with something that looks more coherent and decisive. After all, admissions staff want to see strong interest and motivation, so make sure that's how you feel. Don't rush into making applications if you aren't sure about them.

Writing tips

There is no 'right' or 'wrong' way to write a personal statement, but many admissions tutors say that they expect the majority of the text to be about why you want to do the course, and why you will do well on it. Therefore this is the area you should concentrate on the hardest. Some say you should devote at least 50% of the space to this, and others prefer around 75%. The remaining text should be about your interests, hobbies, personality, etc., and your plans for the future.

However you decide to structure your personal statement, it needs to read smoothly and have a logical flow to it. Because of the lack of space, most students break their text up into paragraphs, and some also use short sub-headings. Each paragraph must leave the reader wanting to know more and link into the subsequent paragraph below. The most commonly used structure is an essay-style format, although you don't have to stick to it:

1 Opening paragraph – usually about why you have chosen to study this subject at university, and what interests you about it

2 Your related academic interests and ability, and other supporting evidence that you will do well on this course and at university

3 Relevant hobbies, interests and responsibilities, and what kind of person you are

4 Closing paragraph – about why you want to go to university, what you hope to gain from the degree, and your career plans.

A carefully written first paragraph is an absolute must. You want to grab the reader's attention right away, for all the right reasons. This will then help to hold their attention throughout the rest of the statement so they don't simply skim through it, and a good first impression helps them to remember you in preference to the rest of the competition. Most tutors recommend that your first paragraph should be about why you're interested in the subject you want to study. You won't get it right first time, so let go and turn out as many ideas as you can come up with, however crazy some of them might seem at the time. It's worth writing a handful of alternative beginnings, comparing them with the opening paragraphs of successful previous applications, and then picking your most convincing one after you've allowed some time for reflection.

ANONYMOUS, AGE 17, APPLYING TO STUDY FASHION DESIGN

'It was really hard writing my personal statement. I kept starting it over and over in a million different ways and hating everything I wrote. I applied for Fashion Design so kept trying to write about how much I love fashion. It finally occurred to me to try something different. Once I did, I found a start I liked and it was really easy to finish it. Still, I thought what I had written was a little strange – I was applying for fashion design and started by writing about how music was my first love! But I took it in to class for my English teacher to see and she said it was brilliant. She said something like that would help it to stand out.

'Here's the first few lines: "My first love is music. The way it floods over me, takes away my surroundings, takes away everything. It makes me feel better and stronger in every way. There's a song for everything I can possibly feel - some I have, and some I've yet to find."

'So far, I've had a portfolio request. I can't wait to see where it goes next!'

Many budding writers are taught that if they want their material to be interesting they should 'show, and don't tell'. This is also true for your statement. Admissions staff want to know how your experiences have taught and shaped you and why certain subjects grab your interest, and they expect to read examples that demonstrate your commitment, instead of being given a list of dry facts. Rather than bluntly stating 'I am hard working and reliable', or 'I am interested in politics', you should try to provide supporting evidence for these statements, for example, 'My part-time job in a busy store has taught me the importance of time management and teamwork', or 'Setting up the school debating society has given me the opportunity to explore many topical issues in greater depth'.

Make a deliberate attempt to use dynamic, positive language in your sentences: achieved, joined, involved, goal, experience, training, planning, volunteering, and so on. Likewise, avoid negative language such as: terrible, useless, mistake, hated, never, can't, etc. However, you can include phrases such as 'overcoming difficulties', 'taking on challenges', or 'learning valuable lessons'.

It's best to avoid 'purple prose' – overblown, over-emotive language – unless you're applying for the kind of course where flamboyance is actively encouraged. Most of the time it makes you look pretentious and somewhat insincere.

SYLVIA ZALK, PROGRAMME OFFICER AT IMPERIAL COLLEGE, LONDON HAS SOME INTERESTING STORIES TO TELL ABOUT PERSONAL STATEMENTS.
'When I worked at another university I did get an amusingly slushy personal statement from a student:

'Walking by a babbling brook I saw a beautiful butterfly. Its wing was broken. It made me so sad that I could do nothing to ease its suffering that I shed a tear. At that point I decided to study Biomedical Sciences at this college.

'Actually, someone has trumped the butterfly personal statement. Yesterday I saw a personal statement from a student where she started by talking about her entire childhood, and went through to losing her virginity and how this has affected her as an artist. It was a pile of pretentious piffle. Apart from making herself look mad, the garbled, irrelevant nature of it all immediately disqualified her, as she was applying for a communications course. I'd say keep to the point! Also don't try and be witty. Academics look for a succinct personal statement in my experience.'

Do:

- Back up comments with examples
- Be concise and use plain English
- Be open and honest
- Be prepared to talk about what you have written
- Be selective and pick what's relevant
- If it doesn't all fit in to the space allowed, prioritise
- Keep it interesting
- Keep it structured and use paragraphs
- Use positive and enthusiastic language.

Don't:

- Express strong political views
- Give your entire life story
- Make jokes or be pretentious
- Make up things or lie
- Repeat material you have elsewhere on the form
- Start every sentence with 'I' or 'My'
- Try too hard to be quirky
- Use long words that you'd never normally use
- Waffle just to fill up the space.

When you're writing about leisure interests and hobbies, try not to go for the same things that everyone else might mention, such as 'watching football', 'reading' or 'socialising'. Something a bit more unusual will stand out, such as playing the tuba in a brass band, or learning how to tango. Pick things that link in with the course in some way, wherever possible. You should also mention any transferable skills your hobbies have helped to build up. If all your hobbies are fairly generic try to show that you're accomplished in some other way, such as captaining the hockey team, organising large events, or being awarded the highest grade for playing the piano. This is not the time to mention that you spend most of your free time in the pub or online gossiping with friends on internet messenger services, or taking part in magical fantasy role-playing games.

It's best to explain anything on your statement that stands out. Sometimes applicants have to write about negative things, such as illness or bereavement that has affected their predicted grades, family commitments that have affected their choices, or a life event that has made them alter their plans. Wherever possible, try to include a positive note, such as a mention of your determination to succeed, or that you have gained life experience or re-evaluated your priorities.

If you're planning to take a gap year, you could to comment on this towards the end of your statement. If possible, explain why you're taking time off and what you hope to achieve, especially if it links in with your studies in some way. For example, you might wish to work to help fund your studies, do some community work, travel or learn new skills or languages. Probably best not to mention if you're just planning on sunbathing and partying on a beach in Thailand for the whole year though. Deferral for a gap year is mentioned elsewhere on the application form so you could leave this out, but you should be prepared to answer questions about it.

International students should explain why they've chosen the UK for their studies, and they also need to demonstrate good language skills. This means creating a well-written statement, and providing some other evidence to prove they can study a course taught in English. For example, it might be useful to mention previous travel to the UK or another English-speaking nation, or part-time work as a translator or in a call centre, and so on.

Students who are not currently in education can draw on their working lives for inspiration. Write about your current and past jobs and what you have gained from them as there may be many transferable skills, anything from managing projects to taking the initiative when researching and evaluating new areas. You'll also need to write persuasively about why you have now become interested in entering higher education. If the degree will lead to a career change, explain why this is what you want.

Just as it's vital to open your personal statement in style, it's equally important to close it well. The best closing paragraph ties everything up neatly, reaffirming your interest in the chosen degree and summing up your goals relating to the course. This is a good time to mention how you hope your higher education will fit in with your plans for life after university or college, if you haven't done so in the first paragraph. Again, readers tend to strongly remember a closing paragraph, so you might like to write several versions of it and then pick your favourite one. You can ask other people, such as relatives, teachers, or friends which version they prefer, but remember that ultimately the decision is yours.

USING QUOTES
Some admissions tutors like to see interesting quotes in a personal statement and others dislike them very much. A well-chosen quote can catch the reader's eye, and make a statement unique, so sometimes they can fit well in an opening paragraph, for example. If you're going to quote anyone, make sure you use the correct punctuation and attribute the quote to them. It's also important to make sure that you've quoted them exactly, or else your mistake could leave you looking silly. Avoid filling your statement up with a very long quote, or several smaller ones, as these will take up too much space, and you will have less room for describing yourself in your own words, so tutors won't get enough of an idea of what you're like as a person. If in doubt, don't use quotes.

PLAGIARISM AND DISHONESTY

It's very important to avoid copying other people's work when you're writing, as plagiarism can lose you a place at university. Admissions tutors read hundreds of applications, and can often spot over-used or directly copied phrases, which they do not look upon favourably. Now there's an even more effective way to catch out cheating students: UCAS's Similarity Detection process that employs new Copycatch software. If you're tempted to copy as little as half a sentence or one phrase from another student's personal statement, there's a very good chance you will be discovered. Taking whole sentences or paragraphs and slightly rewriting them can also get you reported. According to UCAS's Beth Hayes, 'UCAS does have very efficient plagiarism software. If the software detects similarities then UCAS will send the results to the institutions that the applicant has applied to, and from then on it is up to the institutions' discretion on what they want to do.

LISA, STARTING A CHILDHOOD STUDIES DEGREE AT NOTTINGHAM TRENT

'It is important that students don't copy personal statements from other people or from the internet, primarily because they will be found out which could in turn lead them to losing a place at their chosen institutions. The personal statement is "personal" - it should be written by the applicant in their own style. This is the only way that admissions tutors get to know them as a person before an interview. If they are offered an interview, they will probably be asked to elaborate on the information they have provided, and it is very obvious to admissions tutors when students are not speaking from personal experience.

'At my school it felt as though those applying to places like Oxford and Cambridge were considered far more important and took priority when needing help. When help was finally given what I had written was completely contradicted and I felt my statement didn't show the real me - I was worried the unis I was applying to would expect something I wasn't. I don't know if this is the case when they consider students though.

We were given a booklet broken down into paragraphs for us to fill in and then convert into our statement which I thought was good. Getting more than one person to check my statement helped a lot as well, as one person's opinions differ so much from another's, giving better input. Finally it is also extremely difficult to fit so much info into the limited amount of space given and needing to include so many 'proper' words!'

Some students lie in their personal statements to sound more knowledgeable, experienced, or interesting. Be warned though, talking yourself up a bit is one thing, but an outright lie can badly backfire. Some institutions might ask for documented proof of some of your claims before they'll offer you a place. Anything that stands out in your application can become a target for in-depth questions during an interview, leaving you floundering.

Don't be like the hapless student who lied and claimed they could play the sitar to make their application to medical school look unique. Yes, you've guessed it, his main interviewer turned out to be a doctor who really was a classically trained sitar player, and asked several awkward musical questions that the student couldn't answer. So, while you might not end up in trouble for bending the truth a little, outright lies can easily catch up with you.

CHECKING AND REDRAFTING

Once you have put together a rough first draft you can start to check it through and begin to refine it. Read it very slowly to yourself a few times, and make a note of anything that you want to keep or change. Imagine that you're an admissions tutor who needs to be impressed when you're reading it. Make sure each different point in the personal statement links together logically, and then try reading it out loud to yourself to see whether it has a pleasing style and an interesting flow. Save each new draft as a separate document in case you edit out anything that you decide you want to add back in later, and keep back-up copies of these files. Keep making changes until you're reasonably happy.

If the word count is too long, you will have to take steps to trim it down. Go back and cut out any repetition and waffling, then see whether you can turn some of it into shorter, simpler sentences. If it's still way over the character count, ask a teacher or careers adviser to help you trim it down – an English teacher might be best at this. You can also ask your referee to write about some of the things you want to mention in their own statement, saving you more space.

The next step is to thoroughly go through the whole document to check the spelling, punctuation and grammar. A spell-checker will not pick up all mistakes, so you have to do this yourself with a dictionary to hand. After you have gone through it a couple of times you can even try reading it backwards, as your eyes might have become tired and this can help spot individual spelling mistakes that you might otherwise have skimmed over and missed. Take special care when mentioning the names of authors, or the titles of articles or books, as errors can make you appear ill-informed or sloppy.

Then get someone else to read it and give you an honest appraisal, or ideally ask a few people, including teachers, careers advisers, parents and friends. Ask them to check for mistakes, to tell you what's working well, and to look for anything you might have missed out. Don't be shy. You can post it on some student websites too and ask for comments, but be aware that it might get stolen (potentially leaving *you* accused of plagiarism), and the advice you get might not be particularly accurate or constructive. If your readers do come up with useful ideas, incorporate them into the statement, redraft it as many times as needed, then go back again and thoroughly check the grammar and spelling. If possible, get some more second opinions and help looking for mistakes this time as well. Eventually you will have your final draft. If you have time, put it to one side for a couple of days to gain some perspective then read it through once more to make sure it represents you and your goals.

> My personal statement was hard at first because my advisers told me that the first paragraph must be spectacular in order to get the reader (admissions tutor) interested, so I wasted a lot of time trying to make the first paragraph fantastic. And the fact that I had a lot of A level revision to do made me forget about the personal statement at times. But when I did finish it I had it checked numerous times for any minor mistakes by my institution so overall I was pleased with it. However I want to say that the personal statement system is actually ineffective in some circumstances. For example, if you want to apply to two different courses that are similar in context (e.g. Chemistry and Biology) you have to generalise your personal statement to fit the criteria. **,**

MAHAMED ABUKAR, STUDYING FOR A LEVELS
AT HAMMERSMITH AND WEST LONDON COLLEGE

FILLING IT IN ONLINE/FORMATTING

You should now be ready to format and upload your personal statement to UCAS. Go to the website and enter your username and password, then open up the Apply system. Copy and paste your word-processed document into Apply. Apply times out after a few minutes of inactivity, so make sure you save your text during this time otherwise it could be lost.

Be aware that bold text, italics, underlining and foreign characters will be removed when you save the text. Even 'curly' quotation marks (the slanted ones seen in some Microsoft Word fonts), indentations at the beginning of paragraphs, tabs, multiple spaces and long dashes get removed.

After saving the pasted document remember to check it all through once more to make sure nothing has gone wrong with the formatting, and tidy it up if needed. In particular look for lines of text getting broken at strange points, which will eat up space and look messy. Make sure you have not exceeded 4,000 characters or 47 lines, whichever is the shorter, and remember that 47 lines includes any empty lines between paragraphs too. Each time you save the document, the characters and lines will be automatically counted for you, so it's easy to keep track.

> ❛ I did my original statement on a word processing program first, made it perfect there, and then just copied and pasted it into the Apply system. That was it really, although I did have to edit it once, but that only took a couple of seconds. I do have to say though, there is a limit on both the amount of lines you can use in your personal statement, and the number of letters. They [UCAS] should use one or the other, because at first I had the right number of letters used, but it went over too many lines. It meant that I still had to delete things out of my original personal statement. ❜

CORINNE RILEY AGE 18, CHEADLE AND MARPLE SIXTH FORM COLLEGE

AFTER YOU HAVE FINISHED UPLOADING

Once the statement's uploaded, you need to agree to the declaration that it's all your own original work. If you're applying via school or college, you now have to send the application to your referee. If you're applying independently, you cut and paste your referee's comments into Apply, fill in their details and send the application to UCAS yourself (see previous chapter).

Print copies of your personal statement to refer to in case you are called to interview, or have to go through Clearing, and need to refresh your memory quickly. They are often the basis for some very searching questions.

After your application arrives with UCAS, and is forwarded on to the institutions you've chosen, you'll start to receive offers and/or rejections (see Chapter 7). You may also be asked to attend an interview, or to do tests (see Chapter 6). UCAS will also send you a welcome letter that includes your application number, personal ID number and username for Track, and the list of your course choices. If this letter hasn't arrived within 14 days of submitting your application, you should contact UCAS.

SUMMARY: EFFECTIVE PERSONAL STATEMENTS

1. **Think who's reading it**. Your statement must explain to admissions officers why you want to study this subject, why you will do well academically, and that you're mature and responsible enough to adapt to university life. At least half of your statement needs to be devoted to your interest in, and suitability for, the course.

2. **Research and reflect**. Take plenty of time to prepare, and make notes before you begin writing. Make sure you know all the course details, and think of ways to demonstrate your interest in the course and generally show yourself in a good light.

3. **Start and end well**. A good opening paragraph will catch the reader's interest, and a good closing paragraph will help them to remember you, so spend extra time working on these areas. Link all your paragraphs together and make the whole text flow.

4. **Pick your words carefully**. Use plain English, employ positive language, sound dynamic and interesting, and provide evidence that you have the right range of skills, talents and experience. Don't waffle or mention unrelated details. Don't limit your chances by mentioning names of institutions or course components that are not available.

5. **Don't cheat, don't lie**. Plagiarism is increasingly easy to spot, so don't risk it. Outright lies tend to come back to haunt you later. Both will lose you a place at college or university.

6. **Keep rewriting**. The first draft always needs more work. Keep editing until it's polished, and read it out loud to see if it's convincing. Putting it aside for a day or so can also give some perspective and show up areas that need changing.

7. **Ask for opinions**. However embarrassing it might be, you need to show it to a few other people. Include at least one person who works in education. They might think of something important you've missed out, or help you with phrasing or getting the word count right.

8. **Check, check, check**. Admissions tutors will quickly spot any mistakes with spelling and grammar. Errors in your writing make you look careless and sloppy, so you must make the effort to look like you can cut it in an academic environment.

9. **Upload it properly**. Cut and paste from a word-processed document into the online Apply form. Don't use any special formatting or special characters, and remember multiple spacing will be removed. After saving, check number of characters or lines, and make sure no errors have been introduced into the formatting.

10. **Keep a copy**. You will need to refer back to your personal statement if you are invited for an interview, as it's likely to form the basis of many of the questions.

CHAPTER SIX
SELECTION INTERVIEWS AND TESTS

Although many institutions now make offers solely on the basis of applications, some universities and colleges still interview students for certain courses. If you are invited to attend an interview, this good news as it usually means that you fulfil the entry criteria and the university would like to know more about you as a person. On the more competitive courses, an interview can sometimes be the best way to stand out and win that coveted place, as everyone else who's applied will probably also have top grades, the 'right' work experience, and a well-written personal statement.

Interviewers will be looking for:

- **Attitude**: interest and enthusiasm, commitment, motivation
- **Intellectual attributes**: able to concentrate and think clearly, pick up new ideas quickly, think independently, be analytical and critical, and apply existing knowledge to new situations
- **Personality**: usually someone pleasant and reasonably mature, who they will enjoy teaching
- **Suitability**: someone who they think is suited to the course, and is likely to do well on it.

While most of the focus will be academic and you must show you understand what studying the subject entails, they also want well-rounded candidates who will contribute to the university as a whole, rather than course-obsessed geeks who stay in their room reading for the next few years. Be interesting as well as interested.

WHAT TO EXPECT

Selection or admissions interviews vary from institution to institution, and from department to department. The list below is therefore a rough guide to what to expect from the process.

1 Offer of interview arrives (usually by letter)

2 Confirm your attendance and ask for more details

3 Prepare for interview

4 Travel to interview in plenty of time

5 Attend one or more interviews, and hopefully make a good impression

6 Possibly sit tests or supply additional material

7 Return home and wait for decision

8 Meet criteria in possible offer, or get feedback on possible rejection.

An offer of an interview will arrive directly from the institution itself, and will not be shown on UCAS Track.

There are several types of interview and it can be less daunting if you know beforehand what format your interview will follow. Most commonly, interviews are one-to-one with a tutor, or you will be interviewed by a small panel of staff, one of whom often takes notes. The usual length of a university admissions interview is somewhere between 15 and 40 minutes, although this can vary. Some centres invite candidates to a background session before the proper interview, where the process is explained to you, and you can pick up some useful tips about what the interviewers are looking for.

You could also be asked to come in for an 'informal' interview, or be asked to do a telephone interview. Less commonly, you may be invited to attend a group interview with one or more other students, or – in the creative arts – to show your portfolio or perform an audition. You may also be asked to bring extra materials with you, such as recent essays or projects, or to take admissions or aptitude tests.

Who is most likely to hold interviews?

Although interviews are becoming less common overall, they are still frequently held for vocational courses, and other competitive subjects, including veterinary science, dentistry and medicine. Oxford and Cambridge colleges frequently interview the great majority of applicants who fit their entry criteria.

When are different interviews held?

Make a note of when interviews for your chosen subjects, colleges and universities are most likely to be held.

- The earlier you apply, the earlier you may be interviewed.
- Oxford and Cambridge interviews are held in December, with the possibility of more in January.
- Many universities mention their most common interview dates on their websites, and this information is often given in the course entry profiles on www.ucas.com.

If you know you're applying to courses where you think there's a strong chance of candidates being interviewed, try not to schedule a holiday during the interview period. Although some institutions are happy to reschedule admissions interviews around exams or illness, or following bereavements, it's unrealistic to expect them to wait for you to come back from that fortnight in Ibiza. If there is a problem with the timing of an interview, let the university know as soon as possi ble so they have plenty of time to find an alternative date.

HOW TO DO WELL AT INTERVIEW

Although it may be nerve-wracking for some, if you prepare well beforehand it can be an almost enjoyable experience.

Confirming

When you get offer of an interview, read the small print and make sure you're not doing anything else on that day, before clearly noting it down in your diary or organiser. Then call up or email the sender of the offer, usually the admissions office, to confirm that you will be attending. Use this opportunity to ask about the interview format, and if you have a long journey you should also ask about how to book accommodation for the night before the interview. Check whether you need to bring anything else with you, such as examples of your work, or whether you should be expecting something extra, such as an aptitude test. If you have any disabilities or special needs, now is a good time to mention this, so that the university can make the necessary arrangements before you arrive.

❛ Pre-university-interview nerves are completely normal and it is OK to feel nervous. Whether you are 18 or 38, the key is preparation. Firstly, this means understanding *why* you have chosen this path, this university and your degree, and being honest about it. Get familiar with the journey, do the obvious things like open days and if you can, go to departmental summer tasters. Plus an informal visit can sometimes be more revealing than planned ones. Try focusing on positives and remember everyone is in the same boat (though some people are better than others at concealing how they feel). Over-confidence can be risky at interviews. ❜

NAOMI ELFRED, CONNEXIONS PERSONAL ADVISER

Preparing

There are some people who will tell you that you cannot prepare for a university interview, but that is not entirely correct. While it is true that you cannot anticipate exactly what questions you are most likely to be asked, there is plenty of groundwork you can still do to help yourself, and make sure you arrive feeling relatively confident. For example you can:

- Arrange your travel and accommodation
- Go back through your extra reading
- Look at tips specific to your subject or university/college
- Pack your bag and get ready to set off
- Pick out a good interview outfit
- Read up on general interview skills
- Refresh your memory about the course you've applied to
- Re-read your application
- Research the department and staff
- Review your coursework
- Take a mock interview
- Think of questions you would like answering.

Most admissions staff will tell you that when students have done little or no background work, it really shows and doesn't create a good impression at all. So where do you start? Perhaps one of the best places to begin is with the course itself, and remembering what it was that attracted you to it in the first place. Go back through the prospectus and course structure and remind yourself of the specifics, as one of the most important parts of the interview will be your enthusiasm for the particular course itself, as well as your ability to demonstrate an interest in the overall subject.

It's also a good idea to recap your knowledge of the department or school you hope to study at, and look at their well-known areas of research and any other strengths. Start by looking at their website. Key members of staff may have written important academic articles, reviews or textbooks, or been in the press recently. You don't need to become an expert on their work, just read a synopsis here and there, or be generally aware of what they do.

Flick through any recent coursework you have completed in the last few months, if you are at school or doing an access course, etc. Is there any particular subject, topic or sub-topic that has caught your interest? You might well be asked about your favourite areas of study, so be prepared to answer questions about them. In particular, you might be asked about wider reading that you've done in relation to your studies, as this shows an enquiring mind and the ability to manage your own learning, rather than reading only what your school gave you.

If you've mentioned any extra reading in your application, you had better know what you're talking about! It's very likely that you will be quizzed on it, and asked to give an opinion. If it's a well-known text, for example, refresh your memory of it, and perhaps read one or more reviews or evaluations to get you thinking about it. Once you've checked through your application form, look at your personal statement once more. You must be ready to back up any statements you've made in it, or to talk enthusiastically about your work experience and interests.

Read around the subject and think about how it is part of everyday life. In particular, keep up to date with the current affairs and look for elements of your subject in the broadsheet newspapers, relevant magazines or journals, in radio or television news or documentaries, or on news or leading industry websites. If the subject you want to study is not one that's available at A level, like geoscience or nursing for example, you will not be expected to answer technical questions about it. However, you will need to demonstrate an awareness of the subject in the wider world, and have a rough idea of possible career structures and current issues.

JAMES HEGGIE, AGE 21, FIRST-YEAR MEDICAL STUDENT AT UNIVERSITY OF BIRMINGHAM

'I have been to three interviews for university. All the interview dates were combined with tours of the establishments. This is all very well if you are relaxed but, if as in my case during my medical interview day, your innards are busy rearranging themselves, this is a bit pointless. I just drifted through looking a bit shifty!'

'I had an interview in Birmingham for Medicine that was the most stressful interview I have ever sat through. There were four tutors in the room and only one managed to smile during a whole half hour. Because I was applying to do Medicine after having withdrawn from another course I suppose my interview was always going to be a bit of an interrogation. My interview was last and this was how they managed to make my interview last twice as long as everyone else's. The general theme of the questions was 'Do you know what you're getting into?' One specific question was about the roles of the GMC [General Medical Council] and BMA [British Medical Association] and by a stroke of good fortune I had used the computer in the waiting room to swot up on this 30 seconds prior to being called in. I had sufficient presence of mind to hold it together in during the interview but on the train home I was just shell shocked. Apparently my performance was good enough for them to let me in though! I was notified of this by email and by a deluge of paperwork.'

Make sure you know exactly when and where your interview will take place, as the university campus might be quite spread out and it's easy to go to the wrong building. Plan your journey and route, and allow plenty of time for arrival. It's not uncommon to be plagued by delayed trains, broken down buses or roadworks, so build that into your plans, and take the department's contact details with you so that you can phone ahead should you experience serious problems. Print off road, town and campus maps if the department hasn't already supplied these. If you are planning an overnight stay, arrange your accommodation well in advance, and see whether the university has any 'student ambassadors' who will meet you and show you around the campus and the town to give you a student's-eye view of the place. However, be careful not to drink too much if you go out on the town, as a hangover will be easy to spot and will impair your performance at the interview the following day.

WHAT DO I WEAR?

It's often hard to work out what to wear for an interview, but for most places you won't need a suit. The most important factor is comfort, as you may be wearing the outfit for the whole day, and possibly travelling in it, but it needs to be smart as well. Most of the time it's best to go for 'smart casual', so that's trousers (or smart skirt) and a shirt or blouse and a pair of newish and clean shoes. Jeans and trainers are best avoided, although if you feel you will be most confident wearing them, make sure the trainers are clean and the jeans are ironed. Break new shoes in a little beforehand, so that you're not distracted by blisters during the interview, and check you have removed tags, pins and packaging from new shirts or blouses. Big, jangly jewellery can also be distracting, and if you have long hair think about tying it back to keep it tidy. If your interview is in the winter months, make sure you have layers of clothing for extra warmth so you don't arrive shivering. Lay everything out before you go to bed on the night before the interview to save time and stress the following morning. Consider buying a new file to hold any important paperwork and keep it tidy, so you don't have to shuffle papers around when you're trying to find things.

A mock or practice interview can be an extremely helpful way to build up your confidence before you set off for the real interview. Colin Sunderland is a businessman who has helped out as a mock interviewer at his daughter's school, and here he explains the procedure and some of the benefits, which include finding out your weak spots so that you can work on them:

'The main benefit is that it is usually the first experience of an interview that the candidate has had and they don't know what to expect. Although they know that they are mock interviews and that I am a parent of one of their fellow pupils, I am still a stranger and they still approach me with trepidation. At the end of the session one hopes that they have realised that the interviews are not as frightening as they thought and more importantly, it is a two-way exercise. They can interview the college and ask questions to ascertain if it is the right establishment for them.'

'The interviews were as realistic as possible. I wore a suit and the interviews were conducted on a one-to-one basis in a private room. The questions I asked were the standard questions. Why did they want to study at this university? What exams had they passed? What exams were they taking? What were their favourite sports and hobbies etc.'

'All the candidates were well qualified and interested in their subjects. None of them came over as an undesirable person who you would not want in your establishment; therefore it would really come down to achieving the best results. I also found that a number of students had visited the colleges already and this had given them an idea of the layout of the campus and its location, etc. This helped them to ascertain whether the college was suitable for their temperament and to formulate a number of questions'.

'However, there were some common weak spots. None of them had thought about whom the leading lights were in their chosen field or which universities received the most sponsorship for their subject. Most of them had applied to universities in London and although I mentioned several times that I had attended a London university, not one of them asked me any questions about it until the feedback at the end when it was obvious that they had been dying to ask me questions but had been to afraid to do so. Therefore it was other factors such as where their friends were going that determined which colleges they were applying for.'

'My feedback was to advise them to research the establishments based on their subject and not their social life. Visit the establishments, and have a good look round and formulate some questions. When at the interview ask the questions. The interviewer will not mind, and in fact it shows that the candidate is taking a lot of interest in their colleagues and place of work and is likely to give them an edge over the competition.'

If you have time, consider brushing up on general interview skills. A variety of books and websites can give you tips on presenting yourself, making a good impression, handling your nerves, using positive body language, and coping with tricky questions and situations. Try *Brilliant Interview: What Employers Want to Hear and How to Say It* by Ros Jay (published by Prentice Hall) and *Perfect Interview* by Max Eggert (published by Random House), or ask an adviser to suggest something from their careers library.

You could also seek out tips specific to undergraduate interviews in your subject at your chosen university or college. Internet message boards on www.yougofurther.co.uk and www.thestudentroom.co.uk are places to try a search or to pose a question to students who have been through the experience before you. Users will be able to give you a rough idea of questions, although you will have to 'think on your feet' on the day as the exact questions are unlikely to come up.

COMMON INTERVIEW QUESTIONS

- Why do you want to do this course?
- How did you become interested in this subject?
- Which part of the course interests you the most?
- What's the most interesting thing you're studying at the moment?
- What qualities do you think you need to do well in this subject?
- What attracts you to this university?
- Have you done any relevant work experience?
- What do you know about this current news story?
- What are your views on this controversial issue?
- Tell me about your hobbies.
- What are your future career intentions?

Try to keep your answers positive and enthusiastic, and don't write them down and learn them word for word or in parrot fashion – in a real interview such answers will sound over-rehearsed and not genuine.

Come up with some sensible questions you can ask at the end of your interview to show your interest in learning the subject or finding out more about the university. Don't ask about things you already know are on the department's website or in the prospectus, or you will look ignorant – ask about something else that's not covered in detail, such as tutorial support, links with industry, mentoring or the scope of project work, or ask about prospects after graduating. Again, don't memorise your questions word for word, or you'll sound stilted to the interviewers. Have at least one or two roughly prepared questions, or perhaps even three, but don't overdo it.

All that remains after this is for you to pack your bag and get ready to set off. Include letters, maps, transport timetables, a copy of your application form and personal statement, a prospectus, extra material they've asked you to supply, and any preparatory notes you've made. Use a small neat folder to keep it organised if you can. You will also need to pack railcards, tickets, mobile phone, cash for snacks and drinks, something to read if you end up waiting, and perhaps an umbrella. Set your alarm clock to get up in plenty of time, lay out your interview clothes, charge your mobile and try to get an early night.

Arriving at the interview

Timing is important. If you're more than 15 minutes early, walk around the campus or look at your notes so you're not hanging around too long in the waiting area. If you're running late for whatever reason, call ahead and apologise profusely (even if it's not your fault), and ask whether they'd be kind enough to wait for you. Otherwise, aim to arrive about 10–15 minutes before the start of the interview, introduce yourself politely to the receptionist or support staff, then go and freshen up. Check your hair and teeth, and straighten your clothes. If you have sweaty palms, wipe them with a tissue. Take a couple of deep breaths if you're feeling nervous and try to relax. Remind yourself that a little anxiety can actually improve your performance during an interview. Then go back to the waiting area until you are called in. Don't chew gum, and be absolutely certain that your mobile phone is switched off.

Remember that as soon as you enter the interview room you are making your first impression. Stand up straight, say hello, make eye contact with the interviewer(s), smile and shake hands with people as they introduce themselves. Try to remember their names, and wait to be offered a seat before sitting down. Try not to fidget or slouch, and if your hands are a bit shaky from nerves then fold them lightly on your lap. Avoid sitting with your arms and legs crossed, and if possible, lean slightly forwards to show interest in what the interviewer says. Try to look keen and confident, rather than disinterested, cocky or arrogant.

☑ TIP

If you feel slightly anxious, try not to worry too much as the interviewers are probably well used to dealing with stressed-out students, and they won't hold it against you.

The interview

Most interviewers are kind, and will ask you a few general warm-up questions. Think about what you are going to say, rather than blurting out the first thing that comes into your head, and take your time. Try to give whole answers, and if possible, avoid trailing off leaving an unfinished sentence. Don't waffle or try to bluff your way through anything you clearly know nothing about, as you may be asked an even more complicated follow-up question that leaves you totally floundering.

It's quite possible that an interviewer will ask you a question that you don't fully understand or have an answer to. If so, don't be scared to ask them to repeat the question, or to explain part of it to you. If it's a topic you haven't studied yet, be honest and say so. Sometimes there is no 'right' or 'wrong' answer to a question, and they are simply interested in finding out the way you approach a problem and think it through, or how well you can understand the complex components of an issue. Sometimes the best answer comes in two parts: what you think about something, followed by an explanation of your opinions. If the interviewer questions your opinion, be prepared to defend it logically as this is where you might score bonus points.

Remember that the interviewers are not trying to 'trick' you, or humiliate you – but do be prepared for some tougher questions to come later. They may wish to see how you react under pressure, and how well you are concentrating. Just take your time and try not to get flustered. Sometimes the interviewers might prompt you a little if you slow down or get slightly stuck during an answer. But don't worry, this can often be a good sign and suggests they want to hear more of what you have got to say. You will probably be asked about some of your hobbies, interests and extra-curricular activities too, because they're looking for personality and character as well. Remember to be enthusiastic when talking about them.

> ☑ **TIP**
> If you are being interviewed by more than one person, make eye contact mainly with the person who has asked you the most recent question.

The end of the interview

The end of the interview is a good opportunity to ask some of the questions you researched earlier. Try to keep it academic, rather than social if you can, to show interest in the department and the course. Once this is over, take your cues from the interviewers, who will probably say goodbye and thank you and show you out. Make sure that you say 'thank you' as well before you leave.

Telephone interviews

If you are offered a telephone interview, take it as seriously as if you'd been invited to attend an interview in person. Start by doing your background research as mentioned earlier in this chapter, and have your personal statement and a few questions ready. Find somewhere quiet to take the call so that you won't be interrupted, and make sure there's as little background noise as possible. Although you can't impress the interviewer's eyes with a smart outfit or clever use of body language, you can still use a number of tricks to create a good impression: sit up straight in a chair, have your paperwork arranged tidily on a table or desk in front of you, and smile from time to time (it can improve the tone of your voice and helps you to relax). Don't drink, smoke, snack or chew gum. Take your time when answering any questions, think things through before speaking, and ask first if there's anything you don't understand. However nervous you are, try to speak up and avoid talking in a monotonous voice. Say 'thank you' for the interviewer's time at the end, and let them be the first to hang up. You may find it useful to jot down a few notes about the conversation after the interview is over.

Informal interviews

Some interviews are described as 'informal', in that they are not meant to appear intimidating, but you should be aware that your performance in an informal interview can affect your chances of being offered a place. It's better to take it seriously, so re-read your course information and application, and prepare some questions beforehand. Informal interviews sometimes take place during open days and tours of departments, and are an excellent opportunity to find out more about an institution.

Martin Thompson, Head of Initial Teacher Training at the Pilgrim Partnership in Bedfordshire, gives some tips on what interviewers might be looking out for:

'On an application form we would want to see all the details asked for, well presented with good use of standard English (remember the use of ICT is an important skill for teaching so if electronically presented it should show their competence/expertise with this). We also look for genuine interest in working with/being around children who are not family members, i.e. brownie leader, football coach, etc., because experience in schools is not always easy to achieve, whereas such activities are open to all (suitable) interested parties. Also, teachers have to be prepared to give of themselves and such voluntary work is a good indicator of this.'

'During an interview they must try to engage with the panel, be suitably (but not alarmingly) enthusiastic, and concise in their answers (weaker ones often tend to be too long and ramble). We look for flexibility and no hint of awkwardness (I thought this would happen, I didn't expect, etc.), and in needing team players we are looking for people who get on with others, particularly with fellow candidates. The ability to be self-reflective, concisely, is important. We ask what they will enjoy most and what they will enjoy least as part of testing whether they have a realistic view of the profession. Also answers to what being part of a profession, rather than just a job, means are often not good and very few can express how being in a profession might show itself within the ordinary working day.'

'If they ask questions when prompted at the end, which we like and encourage, the questions shouldn't be about things they should already know, or could have found out. We also worry a bit about those who, once they have accepted a place, make too many phone calls etc. asking for sometimes rather petty things. There is a tendency for trainees from recent years to be very demanding, and you would expect them to be able to deal with some of these requests themselves, so they can be inadvertently giving negative indicators of their potential.'

SPECIFIC INSTITUTIONS AND COURSES

- If you're applying for Medicine, Law, or other vocational courses then expect to be asked questions about your work experience, and anything else that shows your understanding of, and commitment to, a future career.
- Modern language interviews are often conducted entirely or partly in that language to assess your general conversational skills and vocabulary, and you might be asked to take a written grammar test as well.
- Applicants to Oxford or Cambridge can expect two or three interviews, which may include an extra interview at a college to which they didn't apply. If they don't get into their college of choice they may be recalled for interview and/or placed in a pool of applicants for spare places.

OWE CARTER RECENTLY GRADUATED FROM OXFORD WITH A LAW DEGREE
'I went for interview to read Law at a certain Oxford college. I had to sit entrance exams before the interviews. I'd had a rather nasty accident the weekend immediately prior to the exams, and was on a liquid diet when I sat

them. The upshot of this was that my school sent a covering letter with my exams, explaining that my performance may have been affected accordingly.
'

'I was invited to my first choice college to attend two interviews some weeks later. As these were spread over two days, with the possibility of being invited to a second or third choice college thereafter, I was offered accommodation in the college for my stay. The building I stayed in was fairly modern, with lights that switched on in the kitchen and corridor areas when you opened the doors (coming from a comprehensive school in South Wales, I am very easily impressed). By contrast, the interviews were held in grandiose rooms lined with volumes upon volumes of books, in an attractive 18th-century quadrangle. This was admittedly a little intimidating. By "a little", I of course mean "a lot"'.
'

'My terror (yes, it's fair to say that it was terror) was mostly assuaged by my first interviewer, who was warm and engaging. I did remain a little edgy, however - as a younger, sharp-featured lady perched nearby in watchful silence. The fellow excitedly enquired about my accident - how it happened, and whether I was going to pursue legal action. Although I wouldn't recommend running into a tensed wire to anyone, it did occur to me that it might prove to be a blessing - albeit a remarkably painful one. And indeed, talking about it would subsequently eclipse the majority of time given for both interviews.'

'Towards the end of the first interview, I was given a handout which documented (to the best of my recollection) a few situations in which an action might arise, and I was asked to comment on who - if anybody - might be at fault. As I hadn't studied Law, I wasn't expected to know the answers - it was presumably to assess my deductive reasoning. As the interview seemed to be coming to a close, the sharp-featured lady unexpectedly shot a question at me, and I was lucky to have internalised my resultant shriek. She asked me whether a confession was ever adequate to convict someone of an offence. At this point, any composure I may have previously clasped to left my body as if water from a colander. I stammered that I didn't believe it was, but didn't really convince myself with the argument that followed. I left the room thinking I'd thrown it all away in the dying minute.'

'The second interview the following day was with a grand old professor in a room which mirrored the first. He was a friendly old stick, and also asked about my accident with almost ghoulish intrigue. I almost managed to bleat on about it for the entire duration of the interview. With 10 minutes left to go, he handed me a piece of paper with about six similar but distinct words on it, and asked me to define each and distinguish between them. I cannot remember what the words were, but I do remember thinking that they weren't as complicated as one might expect from an Oxford entrance interview. I may have hesitated a little, thinking this was some kind of trick. But the prof seemed very happy with the distinctions that I made. I left a little baffled by this. It only occurred to me later why I'd been asked this. I guess that it's possible for people to cram a good deal of high concept stuff into their heads before setting off for interview or sitting an exam... But that's no good to anyone if they haven't grasped the basics. I suppose the examinations had tested my ability to walk; the professor simply wanted to know if I could crawl.'

'I wasn't invited for an interview at any other colleges, and - if I'm honest - left feeling like I'd entirely fluffed my interviews. About a week later, I got an unconditional offer for my first choice college in the post.'

AFTER THE INTERVIEW

Once you're off the premises, make a few notes on the way home. Try to remember who you spoke with, what questions they asked, and how you replied. If you have other interviews coming up, reflect on the experience and consider how you might learn from it and improve your interview technique.

If you weren't happy with one of your answers, don't start beating yourself up about it – interviewers will not reject you on the basis of one answer that wasn't 'perfect'. They will also be taking into account your other answers, your application, your reference and your personal statement, so don't worry too much. If you're really concerned, discuss it with a careers adviser or a tutor.

The next thing you have to do is wait. Keep an eye out for emails and letters concerning offers, invitations for more interviews, or rejections. See Chapter 7 for how to handle any of these, including how to ask for feedback if things didn't go so well.

REBECCA VAFEAS, AGE 19, CURRENTLY ON A GAP YEAR
'I received letters through the post about interviews. Most places wanted me to fill in a form and send that back with a passport

photo (I applied for Acting and Theatre courses, most of them like to have photos on record). One place didn't need confirmation, they just assumed you'd be there unless you rang up to say otherwise.'

'Because I'd applied for Acting and Theatre, there was loads to prepare. Everywhere wanted monologues and some places wanted a song and a written piece. I just made sure I knew exactly what I was doing. You need to be confident when it comes to auditioning for places otherwise you haven't got a chance. Everyone gets nervous before things like that, even just a regular uni interview. The rest of your life depends on how you do in that 10 minutes. But you just need to relax and take it as it comes. The whole thing is nerve wracking. You have to be prepared for anything they might ask you. The interviewers I had ranged from one person to five. They'll always ask you why you've chosen that subject. Some places asked what I planned on doing after taking the degree. My answer was I wasn't sure, I was leaving my options open because three years is a long time and things change.'

'I got a re-call for Manchester Met [MMU] which was originally my first choice but didn't get in. Though they did offer me an audition for Contemporary Theatre and Performance, saying they thought I was more suited for that. Same thing with Uclan [University of Central Lancashire], I didn't get in but they suggested I tried Contemporary Theatre instead. So I re-applied for both. I'd originally looked at Contemporary Theatre at Uclan when I applied, but I didn't think I was up to it, but they offered me a place there and then at my interview. I didn't bother going to the MMU interview.'

'The only place that gave me feedback was Cumbria uni. Nowhere else did. Acting departments never let you know what they thought, which can get frustrating when you keep getting turned down, but it's something you just have to keep at if you want it that much. It works out in the end. I'm off to do a course I never thought I'd be able to do and I can't wait for it. That was my second time round applying. I applied last year and got nowhere. Acting and Theatre really are the worst things you can apply for. Especially if you go for the big well-known places. Each course only has 20-25 places, so you really have to stand out.'

ADMISSIONS TESTS

It's becoming increasingly common to be asked to supply additional information, or to take tests before, during or after admissions interviews. They vary from course to course and institution to institution, but can take the form of any of the following:

- A critique or questions on an article or passage of text
- A drawing or sketching test
- An audition or performance
- English language or numeracy tests
- Formal tests
  - BioMedical Admissions Test
  - English Literature Admissions Test
  - Graduate Medical Schools Admissions Test
  - History Aptitude Test
  - Modern and Medieval Languages Test
  - National Admissions Test for Law
  - Philosophy, Politics and Economics Admissions Test
  - Sixth Term Examinations Papers
  - Thinking Skills Assessment
  - UK Clinical Aptitude Test
- Questionnaires
- Sending in copies of recent coursework, such as essays, artwork, projects or reviews
- Writing one or more essays for admissions tutors to support your application
- Written tests for students from non-standard academic backgrounds.

The more competitive or specialist a course, the more likely it is that applicants will be asked to take additional testing. To find out more about which universities and colleges require applicants to provide materials or take tests, see the comprehensive list in *Degree Course Offers* by Brian Heap (published by Trotman), which is updated annually. The author also suggests checking the details with prospectuses, departmental websites and admissions tutors as they are subject to change, and some of them have closing dates. You can also use the UCAS *Big Guide* to check up on admissions tests you might have to take.

If you are asked to sit tests as part of the admissions process, check out uni websites to find out if they have practice tests that you can take before you go. Speak to undergraduates who are already on the course about the test – you could do this on a departmental open day or summer taster courses. If you have specific requirements (such as support for dyslexia) make sure the universities know this so they can make reasonable adjustments accordingly. Look at online practices and preparation tips for medical degree tests (BMAT/UKCAT) and for Law tests (LNAT). **'**

NAOMI ELFRED, CONNEXIONS PERSONAL ADVISER

The big question with testing is whether there's anything you can do to improve your chances of getting a high score. This depends very much on the type of test, and, if it's a written exam or on-screen test, whether or not you can see past papers (try the websites given below). With something like drawing or performance, it's a case of practice makes perfect, and trying to relax and project confidence on the day. For subject-specific tests that are knowledge based you can take some time to revise the subjects. Assessments for thinking skills and decision making are harder to prepare for, but you can still try to find past papers, and remember to manage your time well during the exam so that you can answer all the questions well and without rushing. Specific test information is given below.

BioMedical Admissions Test (BMAT)

- www.bmat.org.uk
- For entry to some medical and veterinary schools including the University of Cambridge, Imperial College London, University of Oxford Medical School, Royal Veterinary College, and University College London.
- A two-hour test administered by Cambridge Assessment.
- Applicants must register before the last week of September, and the test is at the end of October.

English Literature Admissions Test (ELAT)

- www.elat.org.uk
- A 90-minute test, administered by Cambridge Assessment, for entry to English courses at the University of Oxford.
- Entries required by late September, and the test is taken at the end of October.

Graduate Medical Schools Admissions Test (GAMSAT)

- Entry is online via www.gamsatuk.org
- Required for the four-year graduate-entry medical or dental schools at St George's, University of London, the University of Nottingham at Derby, the University of Wales Swansea and the Peninsula Dental School, and the five-year degree at the Peninsula Medical School.
- A five-and-half-hour test in the third week of September (you must enter by the second week of August), with a fee of £188.00.
- Results are available approximately in six to seven weeks after the test date.

History Aptitude Test (HAT)

- www.history.ox.ac.uk/prosundergrad/applying/hat_introduction.htm
- For entry to single or dual honours degrees in modern history at the University of Oxford.
- The HAT is a two-hour test, and requires candidates to read two extracts and answer a total of four questions about them.
- It is a test of skills, not substantive historical knowledge.
- Applicants applying through their school need to send a special test declaration form in addition to the Oxford application form – they take the test at their own school or college.
- Mature candidates and international candidates are required to complete a test centre declaration form to inform Oxford University where they will be taking the test.

Modern and Medieval Languages Test (MML)

- www.mml.cam.ac.uk/prospectus/undergrad/applying/test.html

- For entry to Modern and Medieval Languages degrees at the University of Cambridge.
- The test is taken in the college in which students are being interviewed, while they are in Cambridge for their interview.

National Admissions Test for Law (LNAT)

- www.lnat.ac.uk
- For entry to a number of law schools: Birmingham, Bristol, Cambridge, Durham, Exeter, Glasgow, King's College London, Manchester Metro-politan University, Nottingham, Oxford, and University College London.
- A two-hour test, the date of which is booked during registration, and the fee for UK and European Union (EU) centres is £40.00 (or £60.00 for centres outside the EU).
- Entry is via the LNAT website and registration opens at the start of August.
- Last registration for Oxford and Cambridge is the middle of October, and mid-January for other universities.
- Late registration is possible until the third week of June.

Philosophy, Politics & Economics Admissions Test (PPE)

- www.tsa.cambridgeassessment.org.uk/ppe
- For entry to the PPE course at the University of Oxford.
- This test assesses whether candidates have the ability to think critically, reason analytically, and use language accurately and effectively, without having to rely on any particular subject knowledge. Administered by Cambridge Assessment.
- The entry deadline is the last week of September and the two-hour exam takes place at the end of October.

Sixth Term Examinations Papers (STEP)

- www.maths.cam.ac.uk/undergrad/admissions/step
- For entry to mathematics at the University of Cambridge.
- The three STEP mathematics papers are sat immediately after A level examinations, and must be taken at a recognised centre.

- Applications to take STEP should go through a school or college.
- The results are usually part of a conditional offer to read Mathematics at Cambridge.

Thinking Skills Assessment (TSA)

- http://tsa.ucles.org.uk/TSA.html
- For entry to Computer Science, Natural Sciences, Engineering and Economics at the University of Cambridge.
- The TSA is administered during the interview period, and is a multiple-choice test consisting of 50 questions and lasting 90 minutes.
- It assesses problem solving and critical thinking.
- Tests are administered under examination conditions, with an invigilator present.

UK Clinical Aptitude Test (UKCAT)

- www.ukcat.ac.uk/home/aboutus/who-ukcat/
- For entry to many medical and dental schools.
- Registration is online, via www.ukcat.ac.uk, with an entry deadline of the third week of September.
- Tests last 120 minutes, begin in the middle of June, and run through to the first or second week of October.

SUMMARY: TOP TIPS FOR INTERVIEWS

1. **It's a compliment**: If you've been asked to attend an interview then you probably meet all or most of the entry requirements and the course tutors are seriously considering offering you a place on the course.

2. **Know when interviews take place**: Check the information for all of the courses you have applied for to see if and when they are likely to hold interviews. Make sure you are available during this period in case you're invited.

3. **Understand the format**: Find out how long the interviews are, how many there will be, and whether it's a panel, group or informal interview.

4. **Take 'informal' seriously**: It's still an interview and you can win or lose a place on the strength of it. Failure to attend an informal interview can result in an offer being withdrawn.

5. **'Look' smart on the telephone**: Even if you're not there in person, you need to be organised and make a general good impression to do well in a telephone interview.

6. **Anticipate questions**: Think about the commonest interview questions and come up with some convincing answers beforehand. Just make sure it doesn't sound too rehearsed.

7. **Preparation pays off**: Practical details such as arranging travel, location, and interview outfits can help you to look and feel organised and confident. Practice interviews, reading the papers, looking up possible careers, and re-reading the prospectus and your personal statement will help you increase your knowledge.

8. **Think like an interviewer**: They want to see a positive attitude, a pleasant personality, concentration, and independent, critical and analytical thought.

9. **Sometimes there is no right answer**: Some interview questions are deliberately designed to see how you approach problems and work them through, or apply existing knowledge to completely new situations. Getting 'the perfect answer' is less important than your process.

10. **Put tests in the diary**: If you have to complete a formal test as part of your application, make sure you know the deadlines for registering and taking the test, and obtaining the results.

CHAPTER SEVEN

OFFERS, REJECTIONS AND UCAS EXTRA

fter you've submitted your applications it's time to sit back, try to relax and wait for replies from every place you've applied to. Each of them will either make you an offer and perhaps invite you to attend an interview or reject your application. Chapter 6 has dealt with the ins and outs of the interview process, and now we turn to the final decisions: offers or rejections, and how to handle them. If you aren't holding any offers at the end of the decisions period, you might wish to go through UCAS Extra.

UCAS OFFERS AND REJECTIONS

Most students apply through UCAS, and they are contacted about decisions via UCAS's online Track service. To use Track, all that's needed is your application number, and your Track username and password. If you've lost your password, contact the UCAS customer service unit (see Chapter 4).

Some universities and colleges will send you an acknowledgement to let you know that your offer has arrived and they are considering it, but others do not send any messages at all until they've made their decisions. It can be very difficult sitting back and waiting to hear from them, but it's better not to keep calling them – they don't have to reply before the absolute deadline in early May, and nagging them can sometimes backfire, so keep your cool at least until the end of March.

There are only three standard responses that show up on Track:

- **A conditional offer** – you are offered a place provided that you meet certain conditions. This usually means that you must gain certain grades in particular exam subjects, or attain a minimum number of tariff points.
- **An unconditional offer** – you are offered a place and do not have to meet any other conditions. This either happens because they really like

you, or because you've already sat your exams before applying and your grades or equivalent experience were good enough.

- **A rejection** – you are turned down by whoever you've applied to. They are not legally obliged to explain their reasons for rejecting you. Their decision shows up as an 'unsuccessful application' notification on Track.

If you gave UCAS a contact email address, you will also receive an email notifying you of each decision as it arrives. If you didn't supply an email address, you will be notified by post instead. You may also be sent a letter or email directly from a university or college, but remember that the decision is not official until you've been notified by UCAS.

You may be made a joint conditional offer. For example, after applying to one course you may be offered a place on a degree or a Higher National Diploma (HND) course, with the university or college deciding which type of course to put you on after they've seen your examination results. In this instance if you accept the offer you are accepting the whole offer – be careful that you don't accepting a potential place on an HND if you are certain that you don't want to study for one.

Sometimes, universities and colleges offer applicants places on courses that they haven't applied to. They tend to be similar to the original choice, but can be in a different format, require lower grades or include a conversion course or year's foundation. If this happens to you, check with the institution that they meant to make you this offer, and if that's correct, ask them to explain why. Do not accept an offer of this nature unless you have thoroughly read through the course details, had an opportunity to discuss it with admissions staff, and are satisfied that it meets your requirements and standards.

Occasionally, an offer can be withdrawn by a college or university. If this happens the college or university is obliged to give you the reason why this has happened. For example, some universities have been known to withdraw offers if students decline the opportunity to attend an informal interview, or fail to reply to their emails or letters.

 I got rejected from Manchester, Bristol and Cardiff for Medicine (with conversion programme since I don't

have Chemistry) but got a conditional for King's College in London. I heard from Bristol and Cardiff first and had an interview at Manchester so I was really nervous 'cos I didn't think I'd have a chance at getting into King's, then I got an offer there before being rejected from Manchester. At first I was worried about having only one offer but I know now that King's is definitely where I want to be! **'**
KATIE BARNES, AGE 18, STUDYING AT EVESHAM HIGH SCHOOL

Accepting offers

Once all your institutions have decided whether to make you an offer or reject your application, UCAS will send you a letter provided that you have been made at least one offer. They will then ask you to reply to your offers. This letter also includes your individual reply date – this date varies from student to student according to the timing of the arrival of their last offer or rejection. If you do not reply to an offer by the date you are given, UCAS will automatically decline all the offers you are holding. It will also send you a reminder nearer the time of the reply date. If your postal address is outside the EU, you may be given slightly longer to time reply.

If you have a question about a decision, contact the university or college for more advice. Take some time to review and reflect on your choices and options before you finally decide to accept an offer of a place on a course – higher education is a big commitment and you will be spending the next few years in it.

You reply to any offers you have been made by using Track.

Conditional offers are usually based on your exam results. If you accept a conditional offer you must meet the requirements by the end of August that year, even if you are applying for deferred entry the following year. If you're sitting winter exams, this date may be even earlier. If you've been made a conditional offer, when you have sat your exams, your A level and AS level results will be sent directly to the institutions you've chosen.

You don't have to make your mind up about offers until you've heard from all of the institutions you have applied to (unless you have applied for a Route B art or design course, when the rules are different – see later in this chapter). Their deadline for replying to you is supposed to be the end of March, although some can take until the second week of May.

If you receive one conditional offer and the remainder of the decisions are rejections, and you decide to take the offer, you use Track to make a firm conditional acceptance (CF). You must then meet the conditions of acceptance to gain a place on the course. Once you have met the conditions, your decision is binding and you have to take up this place.

If you receive more than one conditional offer, you may pick a conditional insurance choice (CI) as well as a firm choice if you wish. Most people who make an insurance choice of this type go for an offer where the grades or points are slightly lower, just in case they don't do as well as they'd hoped in their exams. If you miss your target for the firm choice, but meet the conditions for the insurance choice, your decision is binding and you will be expected to attend your insurance course. You don't have to make an insurance choice if you don't want to, so don't make an insurance acceptance unless you're completely certain you'd be happy to study that course.

If you are made an unconditional offer, and it's the course you most want to do out of all your available options, you should make an unconditional firm acceptance (UF). You must then decline all other offers, as you've fully committed to attending this course. Congratulations, you're going into higher education!

You may find yourself in a situation where you hold both conditional and unconditional offers, but your first choice is conditional and your second choice is unconditional. If that's the case, you can make a firm conditional acceptance (CF) of your first choice, and an unconditional insurance acceptance of your second (UI) choice. Again, if you fail to meet the conditions of your first choice, you are bound by the rules of UCAS to attend your second choice course, so don't make that unconditional insurance acceptance if you're not 100% sure about it.

If you get offers to join your top one or two favourite courses, you can make your acceptances without having to wait until all the other decisions have arrived. Whether you accept conditional or unconditional offers, you may be asked to send in proof of qualifications gained in previous years, or to meet financial or medical requirements before they confirm your place on the course.

You may find yourself in a situation where you are rejected by all of the institutions you've applied to. If this happens, check to see whether you fulfil the requirements for the chance to find a different place through UCAS Extra or the Clearing process. You also have a number of other options, including reapplying the following year, re-sitting exams, taking a gap year or applying for a job.

NIKKI BRUNNING, CONNEXIONS PERSONAL ADVISER

'If you change your mind about your studies at the point where you've already being made offers by universities and colleges, the first port of call is to speak to a personal/careers adviser regarding your decision making processes and analysis. Why the change? What triggered it? And so on. Then if you definitely do want to study something else, phone the university, explain your reasons and ask about transferring. If you are a good candidate and there are spaces on the new course it might be possible. Secondly, you could reject your offers and go through UCAS Extra or Clearing. This is a risky approach but it is an option. The third stop is to take a gap year, reflect on it and reapply.'

For a number of reasons, including changes in personal circumstances, students sometimes decide to decline all of the offers they are holding. In this case, they are usually eligible to use UCAS Extra or Clearing if they wish.

Other students may decide to withdraw from the UCAS application scheme altogether. This is easily done by submitting their decision via Track. Once they have done this, they are not allowed to go through Extra or Clearing, and should they still wish to enter higher education they will have to make a fresh application the following year.

REBECCA VAFEAS, 19, GAP YEAR STUDENT

'I only got one offer. I applied for Acting and Theatre so I'd applied for other schools separate to UCAS, as well as unis and colleges that were within UCAS. So when I kept getting rejected, I was starting to panic, especially since I'd applied last year and got nowhere, I didn't want another year out. But the offer I did get was for an alternative course, which I nearly applied to originally but didn't think I had any chance being accepted onto it! Wish I had now, could've saved a lot of time!'

'I worked out over the two years I was rejected 17 times. Most of them I found out a few weeks after the audition, though one took over two months because they had all my details wrong, so waiting for that one wasn't exactly fun. When you try so hard for something, it really is heart breaking to hear a no. But in a way, it worked out good, I'm going to a uni I loved the first time I went there for the open day, and I always knew in the back of my mind I'd end up going there.'

'There was only one rejection I took really badly. All the others, I was upset, but one I was desperate to get into. I'd spent weeks preparing and got a re-call for it. The re-call went really well and I met some awesome people there. When I got the letter saying I wasn't in, it was pretty much as though there was no point working for things. But like I said, it all worked out in the end.'

'Don't be put off if you get a no. There's always a reason for it, unis know what they're talking about. And take any advice they give you. If they suggest a different course, don't dismiss it, look into it and seriously consider the possibility that it would be better suited for you, even if you don't feel it right now.'

Route A and Route B art and design

The rules for replying to Route B course offers differ from the rules for the standard UCAS route.

Offers for Route B courses arrive via Track, but they must be replied to within 14 days (21 days for those outside the EU) otherwise UCAS will automatically decline the offer on your behalf. Your reply deadlines will clearly be stated on Track.

If you decide to accept the offer of a place on a Route B course, whether that's conditional or unconditional, UCAS will automatically cancel all your other Route B choices. Your options – if you've applied through Route B only – are: (i) firm acceptance (F), (ii) insurance acceptance (I) (iii) or to decline (D).

If you've applied through Route A as well as through Route B, and you are still waiting to hear about some of your Route A decisions, you have a fourth option. You can decide to keep a place (K) on a Route B course, so that the option of the offer on the Route B course isn't taken away from you by the 14-day reply deadline. This automatically cancels your other Route B choices, but allows you to wait to see the response to all of your Route A options before you make your final decision. You will be given a final reply date for this via Track.

If you are holding offers from both Route A and Route B, you can only accept a maximum of two offers from the total offers, with no more than one choice from Route B. If you decide to firmly accept an UF from either Route A or Route B, all your other offers will be declined and you will be committed to your chosen course.

Oxford and Cambridge

There can be a slightly different format to degree course offers from Oxford and Cambridge. If you are successful you may be given a place on your chosen course at your favourite college. At Cambridge you may also be placed in a 'pool' – which means that you haven't been given a place at your first choice of college, but you might still get into Cambridge. This is usually done if your college of choice is oversubscribed, but you're a suitable candidate and they want to admit you if they can.

NON-UCAS OFFERS AND REJECTIONS

If you've applied directly to universities, colleges or other institutions for entry on to certain courses, they will contact you directly with their decisions, usually in writing or sometimes by email. You will probably be asked to reply in writing to accept or decline, or to return an enclosed reply slip stating your intentions. If you accept a conditional offer and have met all the conditions to win a place on the course, you will be the person responsible for sending proof of your results to the Admissions Office as soon as you have them. You may then be asked to fill in extra paperwork to confirm your final acceptance of the place.

Other application routes

CUKAS and GTTR applications (see Chapter 4) are made online, and their offers and replies system is based on UCAS Track.

WHAT HAPPENS AFTER YOU ACCEPT AN OFFER AND FULFIL ALL CONDITIONS?

Once you've completely committed to a course, and have met all of the conditions that the university or college has asked for, your chosen institution will begin sending you information to help you get ready for your first term. This will include how to apply for accommodation, and other information about arrival, induction, enrolment, payment of fees and so on. There will also be subject-specific information, perhaps including a reading list, and additional documentation may be required for certain courses (e.g. Criminal Records Bureau forms, required vaccinations or other medical clearance). If you haven't done so already, now is the time to apply for funding, course-specific bursaries and so on.

DEALING WITH REJECTION

Not everyone gets offered the place of their dreams. Universities and colleges turn students down for a variety of reasons, such as:

- Too many applicants for the course (quite simply you can't all get in, no matter how good your grades or interview skills are).
- The course was already full by the time you applied.
- Not meeting the entry requirements (predicted grades too low etc.).
- A badly-written application, containing mistakes or inaccuracies.
- Lack of awareness of what the course entails.
- Lack of knowledge about what a related career or vocation involves.
- Not looking interested or committed enough.
- Appearing arrogant or smug on the application or at the interview.
- Poor performance at interview: extreme nervousness or shyness, immaturity, inability to understand questions and give intelligent answers, being rude or unfriendly.

‘ Rejection unfortunately is part of life. Try not to dwell on it but reflect on why, and then move on. If all your universities have rejected you try to turn this into a positive. Don't panic as there are other options including UCAS Extra, Clearing, a gap year, a job to make some cash, or maybe a rethink and going into employment with training or apprenticeships etc. You could always go to university later (and hopefully richer!) as a mature student, but the downside is that sometimes you have other responsibilities by then. **J**

FRASER SHADWELL, CONNEXIONS PERSONAL ADVISER

Being rejected is never easy, particularly if you're rejected by your first choice, and sometimes it comes as a shock. There are often strong feelings of disappointment, anger or loss, and it's better to get them out of your system constructively rather than bottling things up or pretending you aren't upset. Cry, punch a cushion, or talk it out with a sympathetic friend or relative, whatever it takes. If things aren't going to plan then you still need to try to make the best of the situation and develop new priorities and strategies, preferably with help from a careers or higher education adviser. Then you have to move on to the next task, and hopefully learn something constructive from the experience.

Although you might be feeling a bit sensitive at this point, you have to reflect on how things have gone and that means being honest with yourself. Look through the common reasons for rejection listed above – do any of them apply to you? Think about your choices.

If you applied for a highly popular course that's incredibly competitive, and you genuinely think you did all the right things to get in, it might simply be that it was oversubscribed and they couldn't offer you a place.

You may feel you could you have applied earlier, before all the places were filled. You could consider waiting for one year and then applying again the next year or you may want to move on to something different. Go back and check the entry requirements for everything you've applied for, and be certain that you've met all of them.

Are your predicted grades too low for what you wanted to do? It's okay to try your luck with one or two courses, but not with all your choices. If you think your actual grades will be much better than your predicted ones, would you be better off applying after taking your exams?

Do you really know enough about the university or college, the course, and where the subject might take your future career? Are you being honest with yourself about your real areas of interest and talent? For example, have you been pushed into something by peer or parental pressure that really isn't the best subject for you?

Get your application and personal statement checked again. Is it really showing you off at your best? Have you been too modest?

If possible, look at your reference – could it be holding you back somehow?

Think back through any interviews that you'd had, and consider what might not have gone so well. If you have any more interviews arranged, think how can you improve your performance.

If you have a reasonable idea of what went wrong, you can then make the necessary changes to improve your chances of future success. Don't be scared to take a little time out to give matters some more thought. On the other hand, you might be mystified about being unsuccessful with a particular application, in which case you might want to write to the college or university in question to ask for some detailed feedback. Institutions are not obliged to give you any further information after rejecting you, but asking politely can work wonders. Their reply might be a tough read, but be prepared for that and ultimately you might find the whole exercise is very useful in the long run.

Occasionally applicants are mistakenly sent a rejection message when admissions tutors meant to make them an offer. Also, in a few cases information has gone missing from application forms, and applicants have been rejected because they appeared to be under-qualified. These errors were picked up because potential students sent polite emails to their university or college of choice to query the decisions they had received. You can also appeal against a decision, by writing to admissions staff that you are disappointed, and that you're still very keen to join the course in question if there are any places left. This is not guaranteed to work, especially if it's a very popular course that attracts highly qualified candidates, but it has worked for some people.

SYLVIA ZALK, PROGRAMME OFFICER AT IMPERIAL COLLEGE, LONDON HAS SOME WISE WORDS ABOUT UNDERSTANDING THE REASONS BEHIND A REJECTION, AND HAS HELPFUL TIPS FOR RESPONDING TO IT IN THE MOST POSITIVE MANNER.

'The rejection process is pretty swift and painless. It's usually just down to competitiveness, as Imperial is very popular and we can ask for a high standard of student, which we normally seem to get. That's the standard rejection blurb. If a student is persistent we'll pull out their file and try and give them more info. Lack of demonstrable enthusiasm is a really big one, as enthusiasm often triumphs over so-so qualifications. A very qualified student who takes a blasé attitude probably won't get in. In fact any sort of arrogance is best avoided. As an example we ask all students to complete an aptitude test. Some can't be bothered and think that sending a URL to one of their sites will do, but it won't. Crap English is another one, regardless of whether or not they have the required TOEFL [Test of English as a Foreign Language] score. The course leader normally decides who to reject, however, sometimes a form arrives from Registry with a "not eligible" sticker on it, which we just need to sign off. We usually send rejections through to Registry, and let them do the dirty work! The students find out online.'

'A student should react by accepting the rejection, and asking how they can improve so that they can get in next year. Asking about possible work experience they can gain in the meantime is good. We have about 120 applicants for 40 places, and the course leaders tend to remember the people who apply, so if they see that you've taken their advice seriously and are really keen you could get an offer. Students shouldn't send their mums in to quibble the rejection, as happened to me the other day. Neither should students bother to appeal, as that never works!'

UCAS EXTRA

The UCAS Extra service opens at the end of February, and allows UCAS applicants who are not holding any offers to apply for courses with vacancies. Only one course can be applied for at a time, and the Extra service closes at the end of June.

To be eligible for Extra, you must have already used up all of your original five course choices, have had answers from all the institutions you applied to, and have either had no offers or declined all offers (including failing to reply before your deadline and being declined by default). If you have withdrawn from the

UCAS application process, you can't use the Extra service, and will have to reapply through UCAS again the following year.

For a variety of reasons, applicants may sometimes decide that they want to decline all the offers they've been made, so they can try their luck with other courses and institutions through Extra or Clearing. If that includes you, think hard about the decision and don't make it in a hurry. Do as much research as possible and take plenty of advice. It's vital to realise that once you've declined those offers and entered into the Extra process, there's no going back to your original choices – the decision to decline them is final and irreversible.

How to apply via Extra

You can use the Extra service online via UCAS's Track facility. Log onto Track on the first day that you're eligible to start using Extra and you'll see a button marked 'Extra' has appeared. Simply click on the button to get started, and UCAS will forward your application to the new university or college of your choice.

The easiest way to find course vacancies is by looking through UCAS's 'Course Search' function. If there are still places on any courses, they will have an 'X' marked next to them. You can also contact favourite universities or colleges directly to see what they currently have available.

If you applied for extremely competitive courses, or popular and selective universities, and didn't get in the first time around, you need to think hard about the alternatives (if you haven't already done so). Seek advice on your options from your school or college's higher education adviser, or a careers adviser before making up your mind.

It's essential to do as much research as possible before you apply to a new course. Take the time to go back and follow the main tips in Chapters 1 and 2 of this book to help you to decide on the right course and the right university or college for you. The latest edition of *Degree Course Offers* by Brian Heap (published by Trotman) can also give you plenty of useful information. If time allows, try to visit the institution in person or talk things through with someone at the admissions office before deciding. Once you've made your mind up, the Course Search entry profiles on the UCAS website will give you some handy tips about making your application.

As you can apply only to one institution at a time, it makes sense to go straight for your new first choice. This can be a similar subject as your original choice but in a different location, a new subject with one of your original first choice institutions, or a radically different course in a new location. The choice is yours, but remember that during the Extra process UCAS will still forward your original personal statement and reference. This can cause some awkward questions to be raised by the admissions tutors about your commitment to a subject if it greatly differs from your first round of applications. However, you could try to get around the problem by writing a new personal statement and forwarding it directly to the admissions tutors for the new course, so check with them first. You will also have to ask your referee to create a new reference.

JUSTINE, AGE 17, FROM LARGS ACADEMY (SIXTH YEAR)

'I applied for UCAS Extra around two weeks ago because I hadn't received any offers from my universities. I decided to apply for a completely different course as my rejections had put me off my original choice of Primary Teaching so have now applied to do English at Strathclyde University.'

'I think the process has been very stressful and has me very worried because I have been rejected for all my other courses, so I am not being very optimistic. I really want to hear back just to see if any university will accept me but at the same time, I'm dreading hearing back in case I am rejected once again.'

UCAS Extra decisions

Once your application has been forwarded by UCAS, the university or college has 21 days to consider your application.

The university may make you an unconditional or conditional offer. If you accept either type of offer you become committed to the course, which means that you are no longer eligible to make any more applications through Extra. In other words, it counts as a firm choice when you accept, just like the standard UCAS application. Should you fail to meet the requirements for an accepted conditional offer when the exam results come out, you will become eligible for Clearing.

Don't leap blindly at the first offer you receive. Only accept the offer of a place if you are 100% sure that you want to take this particular course at this particular college or university. After all, you're committing to at least three years of your time, and that's before you even think about funding. Don't make a rushed or panic decision.

If the institution makes you an offer and you decide to reject the offer, you can apply for other courses (one at a time) if you have enough time remaining. Remember that Extra finishes at the end of June.

If the college or university sends you a rejection, you can apply straight away to another institution, provided that there is enough time. Contact the new course's admissions staff to double-check the availability of places, and the course's suitability.

Every 21 days the Track system gives you the opportunity to apply elsewhere if you're waiting for a decision and have changed your mind about the institution you're currently waiting to hear from. It's best to contact the college or university first to discuss things with them before you apply somewhere different.

If you only receive rejections, or if you decide to decline all offers during the Extra period, you will then have to wait for your exam results. At that point you will automatically become eligible for Clearing (see the next chapter for full details).

📋 SUMMARY: OFFERS, REJECTIONS AND EXTRA

1. **Check your deadlines**: If you don't reply to offers before the individual deadline you've been given, UCAS will automatically decline all your offers and you'll lose them.

2. **Be patient**: The universities and colleges have longer to reply to applicants than you might realise, so don't start nagging them too soon – it creates a bad impression.

3. **Understand how to accept**: Provided you get at least two offers, you have a number of choices open to you if you decide to make one or more acceptances. Be careful with those replies!

4. **Like your insurance**: Only accept a course offer as an insurance choice if you're completely happy to study there. It's a binding agreement, and while you can get out of it, this process can take a long time.

5. **Get feedback on rejections**: Universities and colleges are not obliged to tell you why your application was unsuccessful, but if asked politely their feedback can often be very useful and constructive, and help you to ensure future success.

6. **Nobody likes rejection**: Acknowledge it if you're really feeling upset, and talk things through with a sympathetic person to get it out of your system. Then you can move on to take some positive action.

7. **Query anything unusual**: University staff are only human and occasionally make mistakes, and sometimes software and computer systems can act strangely. If you're confused or surprised by an offer or a rejection, contact the higher education institution.

8. **Should you appeal?** Provided you are very polite and enthusiastic, you have nothing to lose if you decide to appeal following an unsuccessful application. The worst they can do is say no.

9. **Think before you cancel**. If you completely withdraw your UCAS application, you won't be able to use its Extra or Clearing services. Simply declining all your offers will not have this effect.

10. **Make an Extra attempt**: If you haven't found a place so far, the Extra system allows you to apply to one new course at a time, provided that there are spaces and you meet the entry conditions. If it doesn't work out then you automatically become eligible to use Clearing.

CHAPTER EIGHT

CLEARING

In any given year, a university may have unfilled places left on the courses that they teach. This is usually because some of the students who were offered places didn't get the necessary grades or withdrew their applications. To take advantage of these remaining available places, you can use the Clearing process.

WHAT EXACTLY IS THE 'CLEARING PROCESS'?

'Clearing' is a service run by UCAS for people who haven't been able to secure a place at a university or college during the current year. The process allows students to apply for the empty places that are still available. It starts on the same day that A level results come out (in early August in Scotland and mid-August for the rest of the UK) and runs until the middle of September.

Clearing could be described as 'the final round' of the UCAS admissions cycle, and it's effectively your last chance to find a university place for the current academic year.

Every year approximately 100,000 students find themselves eligible for Clearing, although many of them decide to go straight into the world of work, or to wait and reapply for courses the following year. If you decide to go through the Clearing process you'll be in good company: over 35,000 students gained a university place during Clearing last year, so they made up just under 10% of all first year undergraduates.

Many students are mystified by the Clearing process, but it's actually fairly straightforward once you get started, as we're about to see.

Darren Barker from UCAS says:

> The UCAS Clearing process is here to help students if they haven't received the grades that they were expecting. Clearing is a structured and well-organised service, backed by a knowledgeable team of advisers whose experience and understanding make the process simple to use. Last year, over 38,000 people found places at university or college through Clearing. Going through Clearing doesn't mean in any way that a student has failed. They may have had offers from a university or college that they didn't meet; it simply might be that they applied late, or, they may decide that they don't actually want to go to their first choice university anymore. **,**

You could begin to do some Clearing research long before the A level results come out, to give you a head start just in case things don't go so well. Go back over your original applications and personal statement, think about your choices, and find out about alternative courses and locations that you might be interested in.

MARK FULBRIGHT GRADUATED WITH A 2:1 IN BUSINESS STUDIES

'Not getting my grades came as quite a shock but I didn't have time to be upset or worried, I was just thinking about moving on to the next stage. My friends and family encouraged me and I was happy I could go through clearing. I bought the papers the day the results were issued, looked at websites, made a few notes and started calling institutions that had courses I wanted to do on offer. I spoke to someone who took my details and got the course tutors to call me back.'

'I liked the sound of the Business course at Bradford University; it was what I had applied to do at other places and it seemed like a good choice. Luckily, I was right and it proved to be a good place for me to study. The course was taught well and I made some good friends there. '

Your Clearing passport

As soon as you're eligible for Clearing, UCAS will automatically give you a Clearing number, which you can get from their website using the online Track facility. Make a note of this number. They will also post you a Clearing passport form in mid-July containing the Clearing number, which should arrive before the end of August. You need to keep this form somewhere that it won't get lost – it's the all-important paperwork you use to secure a place on a course. Along with the passport, you will receive a UCAS advice leaflet that explains how Clearing works and what you need to do.

WHO IS ELIGIBLE TO APPLY THROUGH CLEARING?

You are eligible to use Clearing if you have applied through UCAS for a university place in the current application year (and have not withdrawn your application), and if you meet any of the following criteria:

- You hold no offers.
- Your conditional offers have not been confirmed because you didn't meet the conditions (usually this is because you didn't get high enough grades).
- You have declined any offers you were given, or you have failed to confirm your offers in time before the cut-off date.
- Your offers have not been confirmed and you have also declined any alternative offers from the same university.
- You have applied after the end of June deadline (or the start of June for Route B Art and Design courses), so UCAS was unable to forward your application.

UCAS's Darren Barker says that 'UCAS is the only way that applicants can enter Clearing, because they would have to have applied through UCAS in order to get a Clearing number if they become eligible. This number is required by the institutions who are offering places over the Clearing period. The Clearing number can be found on Track, the system used by applicants to check the progress of their UCAS application.'

Done better than expected?

Around 40% of predicted grades are wrong, and some lucky students get much better grades than they were hoping for. If you are one of these lucky people, and you're already holding an offer of a place from a university or college, you might decide to try for a place on a different course. However, be aware that you cannot apply for a new place through Clearing unless the original university or college agrees to release you from your commitment to them.

If you hadn't previously thought about applying to go to university, getting better grades than you expected might change your mind. If that's the case then act quickly. Go to the UCAS website and fill in their online application form which will automatically enter you into the Clearing system. You will then be sent a welcome letter and a personal application number that will enable you to track your application via the website – keep a note of it in a safe place. Next, you'll be sent a Clearing passport.

UCAS, as well as the *Independent* newspaper, provides a list of all the institutions that are offering places through Clearing. You can pick any suitable courses from this list and also directly contact the individual universities or colleges.

Darren Barker warns 'It would be wise not to book any holidays at this time of year. If you don't get the grades that you were looking for, you need to be available over the Clearing period to speak to institutions that you are interested in and ask them questions about the course. You will have to be around in person to answer questions and make important decisions. Even though Clearing goes on into September, it is worth noting that many of the popular courses are snapped up quickly on the first day of Clearing. The early bird catches the worm!'

HOW DOES THE PROCESS WORK?

1. A level results are published.
2. Check you qualify for Clearing.
3. Get your Clearing passport.
4. Research available degree courses.
5. Contact universities and colleges.
6. Institution(s) may offer you a place.
7. Send Clearing passport to chosen university.
8. UCAS confirms your place by writing to you.

NAOMI ELFRED, CONNEXIONS PERSONAL ADVISER

'On A level results day, some of the students who don't get their predicted grades phone us feeling distressed. We listen to these students, empathise and give personal examples. We challenge their perceptions of thinking their life has been ruined. We encourage seeing the bigger picture and help them understand there are other options that may also help. Emotions are strong feelings and will pass. It is normal to feel like this.'

'Students receive practical support from us as well. They should phone the university as they may still have places and still be willing to accept them. UCAS Clearing, taking a gap year, and reapplying are also possible solutions. It is also important that they understand why entrance grades have been set and that they relate to being able to cope with the level of study, so, for some students, post-18 employment is more appropriate.'

DEALING WITH THE STRESS AND FALLOUT

If you got lower grades than you were expecting, it's quite normal to feel crushed, miserable, anxious or stressed out. If you need to, go and have a cry and let it all out. Get some support from a sympathetic friend or relative as well if you think that will be helpful. Then it's time to take a deep breath and start to take action.

Before you think about Clearing, contact your first choice university to see whether they'll still be happy to take you. If you only slipped a grade or two, made a good impression at interview, or there have been personal circumstances such as illness or bereavement, some universities will still admit you onto your chosen course. If this fails, you may still be offered an alternative place on one of their other courses. You should also contact the institution that offered you an insurance place.

If nothing suitable comes up, although you might be feeling stressed, do not despair. Your life has not been ruined and all is not lost, in spite of what you might think. There are still plenty of options available at this point. If you have reasonable exam results then there's still a very good chance that you will find yourself another place. Although this new course might not initially have been your first choice, you may find it suits you very well and it could even be more enjoyable than your original one.

Picking a course and location

When you get your results, and you find that you're eligible for Clearing, take a few moments to work out what you want to do. If you do decide you want to enter Clearing, get enough information together before you start. Go back over what you've already learned about courses that would suit you, and consider your career aspirations and subject choices. Talk possible options through with your careers adviser at college, your other tutors or a Connexions adviser (tel: 0808 001 3219). Think carefully about subject, location and course format, financial and other factors, and rank them roughly in order of personal importance.

- **Subject**. With Clearing you are not limited to the subjects that you originally applied for, so if you've had a change of heart you are free to research and act on it. However, you may wish to try for similar courses in different locations, or slightly different courses at the original locations (for example, if you didn't get in for medicine, you might consider a Biomedical Sciences degree instead). Look for course content, class sizes, and teaching scores. Don't accept a place on a course you don't really want at your favourite university in the hope of transferring to your ideal course later – this simply isn't possible at many institutions.
- **Location**. Think about distance from home, campus or city universities, academic and other facilities and the social scene.
- **Format**. You may wish to consider courses with different formats, such as sandwich degrees (where you have time learning on the job in your chosen industry and get paid for this) or joint degrees that combine your original subject choice with a second subject.
- **Financial**. What are the costs? What bursaries/other funds are available? What's the graduate employment rate afterwards?
- **Other factors**. What's the accommodation like, for example? What do current students think of the course, the department, the town, and so on?

Research using some of the different university guidebooks and website. Look at both the ones that concentrate on academic profiles (rankings, subject tables, teaching standards, research ratings, etc.) and the ones that have an 'alternative' view (social scene, popularity and rates of applications).

It's also ideal if you can look through the latest copy of *Degree Course Offers* by Brian Heap (Trotman/Crimson Publishing). Each university's entry requirements are listed subject by subject, and the book also shows you what course variations are available.

You can also look back through Chapters 1 and 3 of this book for a range of ideas and resources to help you decide on the best course and location for you.

‘ I was not accepted for any of my choices in the first subject I picked but I was persuaded to look at a new subject during Clearing so then I ended up doing a top Computer Science degree at a more prestigious uni. They even asked for lower points to get in! It was a pleasant surprise to learn that not everything in Clearing is unpopular or dregs no one wants! My advice for anyone who finds themself in the same position is do your research and don't be afraid to take a step you may not have seen coming. **’**
ANONYMOUS STUDENT

FINDING VACANCIES AND ADVICE

There are many places to get course information and support during the Clearing period. By far the easiest way to see all the vacancies in one place is by using the internet, and there is plenty of advice and support available to go with it. Wherever possible, make sure you have internet access during the first day of Clearing.

Internet resources

The official list of vacancies is published on the UCAS website (www.ucas.com) so it's a great place to start. The list goes online at one minute past midnight on the day that the A level results are published. Look through for entry requirements and make an exact note of course titles and contact details. There is also plenty of straightforward advice in the Clearing section of the website (www.ucas.com/students/afteryouapply/clearing).

Some universities and colleges also place their vacancies on their own websites. Most will at least include the phone number for their Clearing hotline.

www.scottishclearing.org is the official Clearing site for every Scottish university and college. It also links to www.s1learning.com, the Scottish course directory, to give you a wide range of ideas and contacts.

Newspapers

Many newspapers print supplements containing available courses and contact details for Clearing from the day the results come out until the process closes. These are often also reproduced on their websites. In addition, many have up-to-date and helpful articles and advice.

The *Independent* and the *Independent on Sunday* (www.independent.co.uk/student), and the *Daily Mirror* (www.mirror.co.uk) have official listings of all vacancies.

The *Guardian's* Education website (http://education.guardian.co.uk) has vacancies that are updated directly by the universities themselves.

The *Telegraph* (www.telegraph.co.uk) and *The Times* and *The Sunday Times* (www.timesonline.co.uk/tol/life_and_style/education/) provide general clearing advice.

Helplines

The UCAS Clearing phonelines are open over extended hours on results day and the following two days. Applicants can call UCAS on 0870 112 2211 to discuss their application or get advice on Clearing.

For more specific advice, the national Exam Results Hotline has trained careers advisers to help talk through all the options available by calling 0808 100 8000 (calls are free from a landline). The advisers have access to an online database, developed by the government and UCAS in conjunction with BBC Radio, which gives up-to-the-minute information about course availability. Connexions personal advisers and Careers Advisers are on hand to deal with queries, offering free, impartial and confidential advice to school and college leavers on their post-exam options, particularly those in Clearing.

Admissions staff at universities and colleges can offer you advice on suitable courses and entry requirements.

If you live in England, you can call Connexions Direct on 0808 001 3219 and talk to a trained adviser in confidence about stress or anything related to courses and Clearing (see www.connexions-direct.com).

CONTACTING UNIVERSITIES

Use the resources mentioned in the previous section to look for available spaces, and find out what the entry requirements are to see whether you meet them. Make a shortlist of the degrees that interest you the most, and create a list of questions to ask such as course costs and accommodation.

As soon as you've created a shortlist, start calling your chosen universities or colleges to get more information and narrow your choices down further. Sit somewhere quiet where you won't be interrupted, and get yourself as organised as possible before you start. Have your UCAS number and Clearing passport number, A level and GCSE (or BTEC) results in front of you, plus the correct titles and codes of the courses you are interested in, your phone number, full address including postcode, and your email address. Keep a notebook and pens handy, and charge the phone handset if necessary.

Treat the telephone process in the same way as you would approach a job interview, and try to have a professional and positive attitude no matter how stressed or upset you might feel. Don't eat, drink or smoke while you're making calls. Most importantly, take charge of the whole process yourself and make all your own decisions – don't let a parent or friend call up on your behalf as nobody else knows your thoughts and preferences as well as you do.

So pick up the phone … and be prepared to be patient. Remember that the lines are likely to be jammed with hundreds of students potentially ringing the same place during the same hour. Keep trying and you will eventually get through to the staff at the university's Clearing hotline. They will then ask you some questions to see whether you qualify for admission, and may also pass you on to an Admissions Tutor. You may also sometimes get a quicker response if you email Admissions staff directly.

IMOGEN SALTER IS A STUDENT ADMINISTRATOR AT KING'S COLLEGE LONDON WHO WORKS ON THEIR CLEARING HOTLINE IN AUGUST.

'Universities get the A level results on the Sunday before the Thursday they are released to students, so we can see who has made or missed their conditional offers and update our systems accordingly. When we go to Clearing we have about five to eight applicants for every available place. We are polite but firm so we can get through them as quickly as possible. We always check whereabouts the caller is, and if they have someone they can talk to when they get off the phone, whether that's a family member or someone from their school or college. Don't be scared of us! We've nice. Most of all, act like an adult and we will treat you like one. You can cry with terror before and after you have called us, but while we are speaking on the phone try and keep a handle on things.'

When students have missed their offer and lost their place I would say almost all of them are anxious and 20% will be crying. All of them are very quiet - most of them know at the back of their minds there isn't much chance of getting in. In my first year of doing this job I foolishly said to one girl that she was 18 and she had the rest of her life ahead of her - she replied that her life was over and hung up. I have felt terrible about that ever since.'

'Most students applying to our school through Clearing have higher results - they wouldn't ring otherwise as generally they know our offers are ABB at A level - including Biology and Chemistry. You do get people who ring without these grades to try their luck but grades are the first thing we check so the call ends fairly quickly. For our school, the only thing that will get you in is making the grade. If you don't make our requirements, that's it. It doesn't matter how nice you are, how sweet you are, how angry or sad you are. If you don't make the requirements for the course, the person on the phone will tell you straight away and advise you accordingly. (We would normally suggest trying a different institution, or taking a year to retake whatever is letting you down and reapply. There is no sort of penalty for reapplying in the following session.)'

'Personally I hate it when students don't call up for themselves, and let parents or friends make the call. I had one parent who actually said "but it's our dream to come to King's" rather than "my son's dream" which really rubbed me up the wrong way. Luckily they said it to me and not an Admissions tutor and while I don't think this was make-or-break, it would depend on the person making the decision. We only want to accept people who really want to come to our uni and who'll be happy here - not people who are trying to please their parents or (even worse) have been forced into a decision by their parents (it happens). This is because happier students get better grades and make us look good! And they're less likely to drop out halfway through and make us look bad. Our policy is we will not discuss your personal info with anyone other than yourself. We generally ask the parent/friend to get you to call in yourself. It's much better if you ring yourself because you will be able to answer any questions much more quickly than someone else ringing in for you.'

'You must have your UCAS application number and your Clearing passport number. We're not being pedantic. We cannot find your particular record without it and if your name is, for example, James Wilson or Seema Begum there's a huge chance you will not be the only one and we really can't afford to take the risk of mixing up two records - I don't think this has ever happened, but it is easy to see how it could.'

'If you have relevant work experience then tell us. Admissions tutors will look favourably on anything that demonstrates you are genuinely interested in the course. For example, I know that Dentistry tutors look kindly on people who can demonstrate a high level of motor dexterity -such as model making etc. - as this will come in useful during the course.

'If you hold an offer with another uni and you've decided to decline it, let them know straight away so you can be released. If you are still down as "belonging" to another institution, you can't be considered for Clearing. Don't try to fudge it or lie, we can see on the UCAS site if you haven't been released!'

'If you do make the requirements we will take your details and pass them on to an admissions tutor to make a final decision. The people answering the phones within our school cannot make a decision. We can't even guess what the outcome might be as we don't know how many people our colleagues might have passed through to be considered. You won't be able to talk to one of our admissions tutors on the phone straight away. They are too busy getting hold of UCAS forms and discussing who to take etc. However, it will probably be an admissions tutor who calls you back should you be successful.'

'Ask during your initial phone call for an idea of how long it'll take for someone to call you, and then call in if you haven't heard the day after that. Our Clearing decisions are generally made within 24 hours, so make sure it's easy for people to get hold of you so you can accept or decline the place. We call even our unsuccessful Clearing applicants, so they know they are released. If they call you back with an offer (and you want to accept), you'll need to get hold of your Clearing passport and send it in as quickly as possible. Make sure you take down the correct address and a contact name because most unis have more than one campus and the school you are applying to might not be based at the main one. If you forget to get this info, call them back and ask; no one will mind telling you the address and it's really important. Until your Passport is received we can't accept you, even if the UCAS website is showing that you've been released.'

MAKING YOUR DECISION

Shop around carefully and don't jump at the first offer you get unless you're sure it's exactly the course you really want. Go back through all your preferences and requirements one more time to make certain it's a good match. You only get one Clearing passport, and you can only apply for one place at a time with it. Be certain you're fully interested, as higher education is a huge investment of time and money. If you need a second opinion, talk to teachers or careers advisers at your school or college, call one of the helplines mentioned on page 147, and chat with friends and relatives – but remember that only you can make the final decision. If you need to, call back or email to ask the admissions tutor any remaining questions you might still have.

Darren Barker from UCAS advises students holding offers that 'the most important thing to consider is whether they are 100% sure that this is the course for them as they will probably be spending at least three years on the course. Before they accept, they should do some preparation and research into the course and institution to make sure that this is the right one for them. When they decide to take up a place, the institution will ask them for their Clearing passport (UCAS send this to you, once you become eligible for Clearing). Once the student has sent the university or college their passport, they are well on their way into higher education.'

ACCEPTING A PLACE

Once you're certain that the place you've been offered is the right option for you, fill in your Clearing passport carefully. You then need to post it or deliver it in person to the correct department at the college or university of your choice.

If posting, it might be worth paying the extra at the post office to have the form sent by Recorded Delivery so that you have proof of postage and can check to see it's arrived safely. Remember you *don't* send the form to UCAS.

Once your passport arrives at the university and the admissions tutor accepts you on the course they will forward the form to UCAS themselves. UCAS will then contact you to confirm your place and provide further information.

WHAT ARE THE OTHER OPTIONS?

After starting Clearing, you may find that your grades aren't high enough to get you on to any of the courses you want, the spaces may have already been snapped up if you weren't quick enough off the mark, or you may simply decide that none of the available places interest you. If that's the case, you still have a variety of options.

Many students take re-sits to improve their A level grades in one or more of their courses and if this goes well they then reapply to universities the following year. If that sounds appealing, start by speaking to your school or college tutors to discuss the suitability of re-sits. Be honest about why you didn't get such good results in the first place: were you too tired or stressed, unwell, under-prepared, or struggling with the content of the A levels? You will need to act quickly if you decide on this option, and go through the same exam centre and exam board.

You might decide to go straight into the world of employment, either with or without an element of vocational training. Talk to the careers adviser at your school or college, or contact the nearest local careers advisory service. Try the Path Finder website advice or contact a trained adviser at www.connexions-direct.com, or look at the Directgov website for advice about choosing a career and finding and applying for jobs (www.direct.gov.uk/en/YoungPeople/Workandcareers/index.htm). You could also consider an apprenticeship (www.apprenticeships.org.uk), or going to night school to get more qualifications.

Some students undertake a mixture of re-sits, paid work and/or a gap year abroad or in the UK. To find out more about gap year, start by looking at www. gapyear.com, and asking questions in their online forums – don't just take off without any preparation.

Some universities are now offering one-year foundation courses in a variety of subjects, and these prepare students to enter a relevant degree course when they finish. You can ask Clearing helpline advisers about these courses, to see whether their institution runs them and has any spaces left.

You may wish to study for a degree a little later in life after you have more work experience. Examples of this include part-time degrees with evening lectures, distance learning, and the Open University (see Chapter 3 for more information).

Some helpful advice websites and hotlines are listed in the Further Reading section, to get you started.

SUMMARY: TOP 10 TIPS FOR CLEARING SUCCESS

1. **Be there**. One of the commonest complaints from universities and colleges during Clearing time is that many students are away on holiday when their A level results are published. If something goes wrong you need to be there in person to sort it out, so don't plan your vacation for the middle of August, especially if you're you are thinking of going overseas.

2. **Don't panic**. You need to think clearly and calmly, and be rational. Making a sudden panicky decision about a course or a location could negatively affect your life for many years to come, and it increases your chances of dropping out of university.

3. **Act quickly**. While it's important not to panic, it's also important not to be frozen by fear or be too laid back. You need to get moving. In recent years, the most sought-after places have been snapped up increasingly quickly, with whole courses often being filled during the first 24–48 hours.

4. **Do lots of research**. Find out about alternative institutions and courses via helplines, newspapers, websites and careers advisers. Remember some courses that initially sound very different can be extremely similar in their content and structure, so keep looking.

5. **Be flexible**. During Clearing you can apply for courses that are completely different from the ones you originally applied for. Have a rough idea to help you narrow down your search, but at the same time keep an open mind. Don't automatically discount suggestions.

6. **Be organised**. When researching courses, make a shortlist. Then gather together all your important information in one place (including your Clearing passport number, A level and GCSE grades, your phone number and email) and start by calling the college or university at the top of your list first.

7. **Be polite and treat it like a job interview**. You need to make a good impression and show the people at the other end of the phone/email that you're keen and motivated. Mention all relevant experience and interests that could give you the edge.

8. **You don't have to take the first offer**. If an offer is made, take your time and don't rush into an immediate decision. Call back and ask more questions if you want to, take a virtual tour of the university or school on their website, and visit in person if you think you have time.

9. **Confirm your place correctly**. If you accept an offer, send your Clearing passport as soon as possible to your chosen institution – not to UCAS.

10. **Consider other options**. Not everyone decides to go through Clearing, or finds a place through the process. Your other possible choices could include a combination of re-sits, a gap year, and/or reapplying next year. Other students may decide to take a foundation course, undertake vocational training, apply for a job or even start their own business.

Thank you for reading this book, and I hope it has helped!

Goodbye and good luck with your university applications.

FURTHER READING

BOOKS
Background research before you apply
- *Big Guide* (UCAS)
- *Choosing Your Degree Course and University*, Brian Heap (Trotman Publishing)
- *Degree Course Offers*, Brian Heap (Trotman Publishing)
- *Student Book 2009*, Klaus Boehm and Jenny Lees-Spalding (Trotman Publishing)
- *The Guardian University Guide*, edited by Donald Macleod (Guardian Books)
- *The PUSH Guide to Choosing a University*, Johnny Rich (Hodder Education)
- *The Times Good University Guide*, John O'Leary (Times Books)
- *The Virgin Alternative Guide to British Universities*, Piers Dudgeon (Virgin Books)

Funding
- *University Scholarships, Awards and Bursaries*, Brian Heap (Trotman Publishing)

Gap year
- *Before You Go*, Tom Griffiths (Bloomsbury)
- *The Gap Year Book*, Charlotte Hindle and Joe Bindloss (Lonely Planet)
- *Your Gap Year*, Susan Griffiths (Vacation work)

Interview skills
- *Brilliant Interview: What Employers Want to Hear and How to Say It*, Ros Jay (Prentice Hall)
- *Perfect Interview*, Max Eggert (Random House)

Open days
- *Open Days 2008* (UCAS)
- *Sixthformer's Guide 2008* (Inspiring Futures Foundation)

WEBSITES
Admissions tests
- www.bmat.org.uk
- www.elat.org.uk
- www.gamsatuk.org
- www.history.ox.ac.uk/prosundergrad/applying/hat_introduction.htm
- www.lnat.ac.uk
- www.maths.cam.ac.uk/undergrad/admissions/step/
- www.mml.cam.ac.uk/prospectus/undergrad/applying/test.html
- www.tsa.cambridgeassessment.org.uk/ppe/
- http://tsa.ucles.org.uk/TSA.html
- www.ukcat.ac.uk/home/aboutus/who-ukcat/

Background research before you apply
- www.careersoft.co.uk/higherideas
- www.centigradeonline.co.uk
- www.coursediscoveronline.co.uk
- www.cukas.ac.uk/search/index.html
- www.dcfs.gov.uk
- www.direct.gov.uk
- www.educationuk.org (the British Council)
- http://education.guardian.co.uk/chooseadegree
- www.i-portfolio.co.uk
- www.learndirect.co.uk
- www.qaa.ac.uk
- www.thestudentroom.com
- www.thestudentsurvey.com
- www.ucas.com
- www.unistats.com
- www.whatuni.com
- www.yougofurther.com